FOR REFERENCE

NOT TO BE TAKEN FROM THE ROOM

AMERICAN CITIES CHRONOLOGY SERIES

NEW YORK
A CHRONOLOGICAL & DOCUMENTARY HISTORY

1524-1970

Compiled and Edited by
HOWARD B. FURER

Series Editor
HOWARD B. FURER

1974
OCEANA PUBLICATIONS, INC.
Dobbs Ferry, New York

Library of Congress Cataloging in Publication Data

Furer, Howard B   1934-
    New York: a chronological and documentary history, 1524-1970.

    (American cities chronology series)
    SUMMARY: Includes a chronology of historical events in the history of New York City from 1524 to 1970 and a selection of pertinent documents.
     Bibliography: p.
     1. New York (City)--History--Chronology. 2. New York (City)--History--Sources. [1. New York (City)--History) I. Title.
F128.3.F87   974.7'1   74-3044
ISBN 0-379-00610-3

© Copyright 1974 by Oceana Publications, Inc.

All rights reserved. No part of this publication may be reproduced or transmitted in any form or by any means, electronic or mechanical, including photocopy, recording, xerography, or any information storage and retrieval system, without permission in writing from the publisher.

Manufactured in the United States of America

TABLE OF CONTENTS

EDITOR'S FOREWORD. v

CHRONOLOGY 1

DOCUMENTS. 57
    The Charter of Freedoms and Exemptions, 1629. 58
    New Amsterdam, 1661 59
    The Duke's Laws, 1665. 60
    The Dongan Charter, 1686. 62
    The Montgomerie Charter, 1731 65
    Gaslight Comes to New York, 1826. 67
    A Charter Amendment Act, 1830. 70
    Creation of the Public Schools, 1842 73
    The Creation of the Police Department, 1844 77
    The Griscom Report, 1845 79
    The Amended Charter of 1849 81
    The Immigrants of New York, 1850's. 82
    Fernando Wood Proposes Secession, 1861 84
    The Metropolitan Fire Department, 1865 86
    The Charter of 1870 90
    The Tweed Ring, 1871. 95
    The Charter of 1873 99
    Consolidation Act of the Laws of 1882. 101
    The Brooklyn Bridge, 1883. 106
    Cleaning the City's Streets, 1897. 110
    The Greater New York Charter, 1898. 112
    The Tenement House Problem, 1900 115
    A Poem for New York, 1910 118
    The Port Authority of New York, 1921. 119
    The Charter of 1936 120
    The Charter of 1961 123
    The City University, 1961. 126
    The Harlem Riots, 1964. 130

BIBLIOGRAPHY 135

NAME INDEX. 151

For Mother

EDITOR'S FOREWORD

    This book does not presume to be a definitive history of New York City, but attempts to summarize the history of New York in a concise chronological form, and to present some of the important primary documents, and interesting contemporary writings to the reader who is pursuing research in this fruitful field. A spectrum of facts and sources have been cited to provide the reader with the widest possible coverage of New York's history and development within the confines of a small volume. Multiple volumes can, of course, be written on any period of New York's history. For example, the thirty year period between 1940 and 1970 would call for a series of volumes on each decade, and in some special cases, on particularly crucial and important years. This work, then, is a good starting point for those students interested in pursuing further the study of the Empire City.

    Because the very nature of preparing a chronology of this type precludes the author from using the standard form of historical footnoting, I should like to acknowledge, in the editor's foreword, the major sources used to compile the bulk of the chronological and factual materials comprising the chronology section of this work. They are as follows: I.N. Phelps Stokes, The Iconography of Manhattan Island, 1498-1909, 6 vols. New York, 1915-1926; and I.N. Phelps Stokes, New York, Past and Present. New York, 1939.

                                                      Howard B. Furer
                                                      Kean College of New Jersey
                                                      Union, New Jersey

CHRONOLOGY

When New York Was New Amsterdam - 1524-1664

1524	April 17. Giovanni De Verrazano, a Florentine sea captain, sailing under the flag of France, was the first European to reach what is now New York Harbor.
1609	September 13. Henry Hudson, sailing for the Dutch East India Company, entered the harbor at New York and sailed up the Hudson River as far as Albany. This voyage laid the basis for the Dutch claims to this region.
1610-1618	Following the voyage of Henry Hudson, several exploring and trading expeditions under Dutch auspices were made to the region that is now New York. Adriaen Block sailed to Manhattan (1613), and discovered Hell Gate, Block Island, and other sites in the area.
1621	June 3. Under the leadership of William Usselinx, a prominent merchant, the Dutch West India Company was founded. The charter conferred a trading monopoly, and the right to colonize in the New World and along the west coast of Africa. The company was organized into five chambers, the most important being the Amsterdam Chamber which had immediate control of New Netherland.
1624	March 28. A Provisional Order, the first plan of government of the colony, based in large measure on the <u>Artikelbrief</u> (rules governing life aboard ship), was adopted by the company.
	March 30. Some thirty families, mostly Walloons, sailed from Amsterdam under the leadership of Cornelius Jacoben May, a sea captain, who was named first director of the colony. On arrival in New York Bay, a small group was left at a fort on Nut (Governor's) Island, several families were sent to the Delaware, and eighteen families proceeded up the Hudson. It is conjectured, but not established, that some members of the latter group settled on Manhattan Island.
1626	January. William Verhulst, sent out as a super-cargo, became second director, with a council made up of available Dutch sea captains, a vice-director, and a vice-commissioner.
	September 23. As a result of Verhulst's mismanagement,

the council ousted him, appointing in his place Peter Minuit. Minuit had arrived on May 4, 1626 with a new group of emigrants, who proceeded that summer to erect on Manhattan Island thirty houses. In the same year, Minuit purchased Manhattan Island from native chiefs for sixty guilders, about $24, paid in trading goods, and changed its name to New Amsterdam. Settlement was reinforced by withdrawing settlers from Ft. Orange and from the Delaware.

1627   Beaver and Otter skins and other merchandise were sent back to Holland by the West India Company for the first time.

1628   April. The first regular minister of the Dutch Reformed Church arrived. He was Jonas Michelius.

1629   June 7. The West India Company granted the Charter of Freedoms and Exemptions in order to encourage colonization in New Netherlands.

1630   January. Five patroonships were granted in New Netherlands; Pavonia, Swaenendael, Rensselaerswyck, were settled at this time.

1631   Peter Minuit was recalled by the company, who felt he had been too liberal in granting trading privileges to the various patroons.

1632   March. Bastiaen Jansean Krol succeeded Minuit. Krol acted as Director-General until 1633.

1633   Wouter Van Twiller was appointed Director-General.

1634   Two early settlers, Roeloff and Annetje Jans began a farm on land later to become Trinity Church.

1636   Jacobus Van Curler and Wolfert Geritsen began the settlement of what is now Queens and Flatlands.

1638   The first ferry to Long Island was established.

March. The first school teacher in New Amsterdam arrived. He was Adam Roelantsen.

May. The first recorded murder in New Amsterdam occurred. Gerrit Jansen was stabbed to death in front of Fort Amsterdam.

CHRONOLOGY

1639 The West India Company's monopoly over the fur trade was rescinded. This act helped bring more settlers to New Amsterdam.

The first map of what is now Greater New York was published. It was called the "Manaties Map."

February 10. A farm was begun on Staten Island by David Pietersz de Vries. It did not succeed.

1640 May 10. A militia was organized in New Amsterdam.

July 19. A new "Charter of Freedoms and Exemptions" was issued. Its purpose was to promote emigration to the colony.

1641 English emigrants began moving into the Bronx, and sections of Brooklyn and Queens. Governor Kieft, as a result, appointed a special English secretary in 1642.

August. Indians raided Manhattan and Staten Island.

August 29. The beginning of representative government in New Amsterdam occurred, when residents chose a Board of Twelve Men to represent them. The Board had little power as yet.

1642 A new church was built at the tip of Manhattan Island.

The first two taverns in New Amsterdam were opened. They were the City Tavern (later City Hall), and Philip Geraedy's Tavern.

January 21. Governor Kieft and the Board of Twelve Men agreed to launch a campaign against the Indians of the lower Hudson Valley. The offensive proved a failure.

April. James Bronck, a settler on the Bronx River arranged a one year's truce between the New Amsterdam colonists and the Indians.

1643 February 18. The Board of Twelve Men was dismissed by Governor Kieft when they demanded greater authority.

September 13. The settlers chose a new Board of Eight Men to aid Kieft with Indian problems.

1644	February 25. A group of black slaves were granted their freedom by the West India Company.
	July. Because of the Indian danger, a stone wall was built across the tip of Manhattan, and settlers from the upper Hudson Valley were brought to live within the confines of the wall. Present day Wall Street follows the path of the old wall.
1645	November 16. Additional settlements were begun in Flushing (1645), Gravesend (1646), and Breukelen (Brooklyn, 1646), when Governor Kieft purchased lands from the Indians.
1646	February 26. Peter Stuyvesant was appointed Director-General of New Amsterdam.
	May. The first black slaves to be sold in the city arrived.
	November 26. The West India Company granted Brooklyn a charter providing for a municipal form of government.
1647	May 11. Peter Stuyvesant arrived in the city. A new Board of Nine Men was chosen by the residents to work with the Governor.
1648	The first pier in the city was built on the East River.
1649	July 29. Three men were sent home to Holland by the Board of Nine Men to present a list of grievances to the States General.
	October 13. The West India Company was charged with neglect by the Board of Nine Men. Reforms were proposed including a form of self-government.
1650	November 29. Governor Stuyvesant refuted the charges of the Board of Nine Men.
1652	April. Under orders from the Dutch government, Stuyvesant was forced to grant a city government for New Amsterdam.
	July. The first Latin School was established in the city. It lasted for two years.
1653	February 2. New Amsterdam was proclaimed a municipal-

ity. A Schout, two burgomasters, and five Schepens were appointed to run city affairs.

February 6. The first session of Burgomasters and Schepens was held at the City Tavern.

February 24. The City Tavern now became the City Hall.

March. The first jail was established in the fort.

March 13. A night watch was established, and a series of new defenses were planned for the city.

May. On Beaver Street, the city's first Poor House was erected.

July 24. The first lawyer allowed to practice in the city was Adriaen vander Donck.

December 10. Delegates representing the various parts of New Netherlands met at the first General Assembly (landdag) at City Hall.

1654 August 24. A gracht or canal was constructed on Broad Street, and orders were issued to keep it full of water at all times because of fire needs. Additions to the canal were made in 1657, 1659, 1662, and 1663.

September. The first group of Jews to settle in the city arrived. They were led by Jacob Barsimson.

November 2. Repairs were made to the bank of the East River in front of City Hall. By 1670, additional repairs were completed along the entire East River shore.

December 8. The West India Company presented the first official city seal to Governor Stuyvesant.

1655 The first church in Flatbush (Brooklyn) was erected.

October. The first assessment list ever recorded in the city was drawn up.

1656 February 22. The first Jewish cemetery in the city was established at Chatham Square. Part of it still stands, and is the oldest cemetery on Manhattan Island.

February 25. The first survey of New Amsterdam was made by Frederick de Koningh. It listed one thousand inhabitants and one hundred and twenty houses.

February 26. The first brokerage system in the city was established. Jan Peeck, who spoke both Dutch and English, was appointed the first broker.

September 12. The first public market in the city was opened.

1657 January. The first Dutch Lutheran minister in the city arrived.

February 2. Great and small "burgher-rights" were established in the city. These rights enabled residents to participate in trading, as well as other aspects of city life.

April-May. Jacques Cortelyou made another survey of New Amsterdam.

August 6. The first Quakers arrived in New Amsterdam.

1658 February 14. Governor Stuyvesant built an estate called "Whitehall." It was destroyed by fire in 1715.

March. Harlem was founded. The first settler in this area was Hendrick de Forest.

October. The city established a night police or watch.

1659 February. The first small hospital was opened.

April. The first meat market in the city was opened.

1660 Governor Stuyvesant built a chapel on his farm.

June. Jacques Cortelyou prepared a new plan of the city. It is now considered the earliest known existing plan of New Amsterdam.

July 10. The first city directory was prepared by Nicasius de Sille.

September 22. New defenses and fortifications for the city were undertaken on the orders of Stuyvesant.

CHRONOLOGY

1661   December. Five Dutch and six English villages were incorporated in what is now the borough of Queens.

1662   September 21. An ordinance was passed prohibiting all other religions in the city except the Dutch Reformed Church.

1663   February 5. A minor earthquake occurred in the city.

           November 1-3. The provincial assembly, meeting at New Amsterdam attempted to settle a boundary dispute with Connecticut.

1664   The population of New Amsterdam totaled 1,500 people.

           January 23. The West India Company's charter rights were confirmed by the Dutch goverment.

           March 12-22. King Charles II of England granted to his brother James, the Duke of York, all the territory between the Connecticut and Delaware Rivers. The King regarded the Dutch as usurpers.

           June 28-July 8. Learning of the approach of an English fleet, Stuyvesant and the Council ordered new defenses and fortifications.

           August 28. An English fleet anchored off New Amsterdam. Colonel Richard Nicolls, its commander, demanded the surrender of New Amsterdam.

           September 5. Although urged to surrender, Stuyvesant and the Council announced their determination to defend the city.

           September 8. The situation being hopeless, Stuyvesant formally surrendered New Amsterdam to the English.

           October 4. Colonel Nicolls renamed New Amsterdam, New York in honor of its proprietor, the Duke of York. However, he allowed the Dutch municipal officers to continue to rule for the time being.

           THE ENGLISH PERIOD - 1664-1783

1664   October 20. The Dutch officials and residents of the city took the oath of allegiance to English authority.

November 24. The Dutch officials sent a letter to the Duke of York in which they promised obedience to the new regime.

December 6. Richard Nicolls was appointed the new governor of the province, and permitted the Lutherans of the city freedom to worship as they pleased.

1665

The first church in Harlem was built near the river.

February 23. The English confiscated all the possessions of the West India Company in the colony.

March 1. Governor Nicolls and the council issued the Dukes Laws. They applied to civil and criminal law, the election of officials, and freedom of religion.

April 19. About one hundred British soldiers were quartered in the homes of the Dutch residents of the city, who were paid for the service.

June 12. The English form of municipal government was substituted for the Dutch form. It consisted of a mayor, aldermen, and a sheriff. This was known as the Nicolls Charter.

June 13. Thomas Willet was appointed first mayor of New York.

June 15. The mayor and aldermen held their first meeting.

1666

The first church in Brooklyn was erected.

1667

July 3. The first public ferry in Harlem was established.

July 21-31. New York was confirmed to the English as a result of the Treaty of Breda.

October 11. Governor Nicolls granted a new patent to the freeholders of Harlem under the name New Harlem.

1668

March. Francis Lovelace was appointed the new governor of New York.

May 3. John Archer was granted permission to settle sixteen families in the area that became the town of Fordham in the Bronx.

June 25. The first ferry between New York and Jersey City was established.

October. The first city seal under the English was adopted.

1670
March 24. Governor Lovelace ordered all merchants to meet every Friday near the bridge at Broad Street. This may be considered the first exchange in the city.

April 13. Thomas Lovelace and Matthias Nicolls officially took possession of Staten Island for the British government.

August 10. A patent was issued to Isaac Bedloe for the island in New York Harbor which bears his name.

1671
The first Lutheran church in the city was opened in the home of Cornelius Pluvier.

May. The first Quaker meeting in the city took place.

1672
February. Peter Stuyvesant died. He was buried under the chapel on his estate.

July 3. Governor Lovelace ordered new defenses for the city, as war with Holland had broken out.

December 10. A monthly postal service between New York and Boston was established.

1673
August 8. A Dutch fleet anchored off Staten Island. Captain Richard Manning commanded the defenses of the city.

August 9. New York was recaptured by the Dutch and renamed New Orange.

August 12. Anthony Colve was appointed Governor-General of New Netherlands.

August 17. The city government reverted back to the old Dutch form.

October 16. The Dutch destroyed old Fort Amsterdam, and built new defenses at the tip of Manhattan Island.

1674
November 10. New Netherlands was given back to Great Britain. Sir Edmund Andros was appointed governor, and

the city was once again renamed New York. The city government again became English, and Matthias Nicolls was appointed mayor.

1675   November 24. The English equivalent of Dutch Burgher-Right (admission of freemen) began.

1676   The first Lutheran church building in the city was built.

The Great Dock was constructed on the East River. It was the only place of dockage until 1750.

1677   November 20. The first insane asylum in New York was constructed.

1680   January 7. New York City was granted a monopoly over the bolting of flour for exportation by the British government.

January 8. What might be called the first labor union in the city was organized. It was an association of coopers.

1681   January 7. Because of charges of corruption, Governor Andros was recalled to England. Anthony Brockholls was placed in charge of the city.

1683   January 27. Thomas Dongan was appointed Governor. He was given instructions to provide for the election of a general assembly, and revise taxes.

October 27. The first general assembly of the province met in New York City.

October 30. The general assembly passed the Charter of Liberties and Privileges.

November 9. The city officials asked Governor Dongan for a new charter granting greater privileges and powers.

December 4. John Graham was appointed recorder of the city. He may be considered the first corporation counsel.

December 6. Governor Dongan issued a new charter for the city.

December 8. The city was divided into six wards.

CHRONOLOGY

1684   February 14. The first Common Council of the city, consisting of six aldermen, and six assistant aldermen were sworn into office.

October 13. For the first time, aldermen, assistants, constables and assessors were elected by the freemen of the city.

1685   February 6. New York became a royal colony when the Duke of York became King James II.

March 3. James II ordered the government of New York province be assimilated into the Dominion of New England.

1688   The first French Huguenot church was erected in the city.

April 7. New York and New Jersey were added to the Dominion of New England. Exonerated of all charges, Edmund Andros was appointed governor of the whole territory.

1689   May 31. The Leisler Rebellion, an uprising in the city against the rule of James II, began.

August 16. Jacob Leisler, a German, was appointed commander-in-chief of the province, by a Committee of Public Safety in New York.

October 14. Peter Delanoy was elected mayor of the city, the first person ever elected to that post.

1691   March 20. By this time, William and Mary had come to the throne in England. Henry Slaughter, the newly arrived governor, arrested Jacob Leisler.

May 16. Leisler and Jacob Milbourne were hanged for treason.

June 23. Governor Slaughter died, and the Council temporarily chose Richard Ingoldsby to replace him.

1692   The South Dutch Church was constructed.

April 30. Benjamin Fletcher, the new governor, arrived.

1693   King's Bridge was built. It was the first bridge across the Harlem River.

1697	May 6. Trinity Church was incorporated.
	November 23. The first oil lamps were placed on the city's streets.
1698	March 13. Trinity Church was opened and dedicated.
	April 2. Benjamin Fletcher was succeeded by the Earl of Bellomont as governor.
1699	Construction began on a second City Hall at Wall and Nassau Streets. It was completed in 1704.
1702	May 3. Edwin Hyde, (Lord Cornbury), replaced the Earl of Bellomont as governor.
	July. A severe epidemic raged through the city.
1703	New York City's population reached 4,436.
	April 22. Trinity Church was granted the old cemetery on Broadway by the Common Council.
1705	November 23. Trinity Church received the old Queen's Farm and Garden from Lord Cornbury.
1707	January. A group of Scottish immigrants introduced Presbyterianism into the city.
1708	December 18. Cornbury was replaced as governor by Lord John Lovelace.
1709	May 6. Governor Lovelace died, and Richard Ingoldsby again temporarily took charge.
1710	June 14. Robert Hunter was appointed the new governor. Many Palatine Germans, whom he brought with him, settled in the city.
1712	April 7-21. A Negro insurrection broke out in the city. It was put down by Governor Hunter.
1713	April 2. The first public ferry between New York and Staten Island was established.
1720	September 17. Hunter was replaced by William Burnet as governor.

1723	New York's population stood at 7,248.
1725	November 1. William Bradford issued the first newspaper published in the city. It was the New York Gazette.
1728	The first Baptist Church in the city was built.
	April 15. John Montgomerie replaced William Burnet as governor.
1729	The first Jewish synagogue in the city was built on Mill Street.
1731	February 11. Governor Montgomerie granted a new charter for the city. It gave city officials more powers.
	July 1. Governor Montgomerie died, and the Common Council took charge of city government.
	November 21. The city received its first two fire engines from England.
1732	August 1. William Cosby was appointed the new governor.
	December 6. The first theater in New York City opened in a building owned by Rip Van Dam.
1733	March. A Bowling Green was opened on land at the lower end of Broadway.
1735	The first City Almshouse was opened in what is now City Hall Park.
	August 4. John Peter Zenger, editor of the New York Weekly Journal, was tried for libel of Governor Cosby, and acquitted. Freedom of the press received a big boost from this trial.
1736	March 10. Governor Cosby died, and was temporarily replaced by George Clark, the president of the provincial council.
1737	The population of New York City was 10,664.
1738	June 28. A quarantine on all incoming ships, until visited by a city physician, was ordered by the Common Council.

September 19. The first organized volunteer fire department in the city was established.

1741 February 28. The so-called Negro Plot to burn the city began.

By October 22, 1742, thirty-two blacks were executed, seventy-one were shipped out of the city, and three whites were hanged.

1743 September 22. George Clinton, the newly appointed governor, arrived.

1744 May 3. The Common Council passed a series of ordinances designed to improve health and sanitary conditions in the city.

1747 April 2. Large groups of skilled workers protested to Governor Clinton against the low wage scale being introduced into the city by workmen from neighboring colonies.

1750 April. Docks were constructed at Hunter's Key.

1753 October 7. Sir Danvers Osborn succeeded George Clinton as governor.

October 12. Governor Osborn committed suicide, and was temporarily replaced by Lieutenant-Governor DeLancey.

1754 April 8. The New York Society Library, the oldest library in the city, was founded.

October 31. King's College (Columbia) was chartered, and Samuel Johnson was appointed its first president.

1755 September 2. Sir Charles Hardy, the new governor, arrived in New York.

1757 The first history of New York City was published in London by William Smith.

1758 A pesthouse was constructed on Bedloes Island.

1759 October 1. A new jail was built on the Commons, and all prisoners were removed from City Hall Jail and sent to the new building.

October 12. New York City celebrated General James Wolfe's victory over the French at Quebec.

1760   July 20. Lieutenant-Governor DeLancey died. Cadwallader Colden, the oldest member of the provincial council now took charge of the city's affairs.

1761   October 19. Robert Monckton was appointed the new governor.

1762   The first lamp posts with oil lamps were placed on the city's streets.

1763   New York's population reached 12,000, while the city was divided into seven wards.

1765   October 7-25. The Stamp Act Congress met at City Hall.

October 22. The first stamps under the Stamp Act were secretly landed at New York City and placed in the City Hall.

October 31. New York merchants adopted a non-importation agreement until the Stamp Act was repealed.

November 1. A mob marched on City Hall to protest the Stamp Act, and the placement of the stamps in that building.

November 13. Sir Henry Moore was appointed the new governor.

1766   The first Methodist services in the city were held at the home of Philip Embury.

May 20. New Yorkers celebrated the repeal of the Stamp Act. They erected a liberty pole on the Commons.

August 11. English soldiers cut down the liberty pole on the Commons. A fight broke out between New York Sons of Liberty and the English soldiers. A new pole was put up the next day.

October 30. St. Paul's Chapel was opened.

December 7. The John Street Theater was opened.

1768	The Presbyterians opened their newly completed Brick Church.
	April 5. The New York Chamber of Commerce was organized.
1770	January 19. New Yorkers and British soldiers came to blows at the so-called Battle of Golden Hill.
	August 16. An equestrian statue of George III was erected on Bowling Green.
	September 7. A statue of William Pitt was erected on Wall Street.
	October 18. The Earl of Dunmore was appointed the new governor.
1771	The population of the city reached 21,863.
	May 28. The New York Hospital, the oldest in the city, was incorporated.
	July 8, William Tryon succeeded Lord Dunmore as governor.
1774	April 22. New Yorkers staged their own "tea party" when tea on board the ship London was thrown into the harbor.
	Christopher Colles made the first recorded proposal that the city government create a water supply. The suggestion was accepted by the Common Council, and a reservoir was built on the east side of Broadway, between Franklin and White Streets. The project was interrupted by the Revolution, and although Colles and others sought to revive it, no water supply was furnished until after the organization of the private Manhattan Company in 1799. Up to that time, the city's supply of drinking water was derived from wells, the most important of which was the famous Tea Water Pump at Chatham and Pearl Streets, or from private water vendors.
1775	February. The Bridewell was erected in City Hall Park.
	April 23. A general uprising took place in New York when news of the battles of Lexington and Concord arrived. New

Yorkers took possession of government arms, distributed them to citizens, and formed a Voluntary Corps which assumed control over the government.

May 23. The first provincial Congress met in New York City. It planned new defenses and authorized the enlistment of troops.

October 19. Governor Tryon fled the city.

1776

February 4. General Charles Lee supervised the construction of new defenses for the city.

April 13. General George Washington arrived in the city to take command of its defense against the British.

July 9. The Declaration of Independence was read to New Yorkers, who then pulled down the statue of George III in Bowling Green Park.

August 27. The British defeated the Americans at the Battle of Long Island. Washington moved his army to Manhattan.

September 15. The British landed at Kip's Bay, and captured New York City.

September 21. A great fire broke out in the city, which destroyed Trinity Church and a large number of other buildings.

September 22. Nathan Hale was executed as a spy by the British in New York City.

November 16. The British occupied all of Manhattan Island. Military government was installed, and remained in control of the city until the British evacuation in 1783.

1778

August. Another disastrous fire destroyed about one hundred buildings in the city.

1780

March 21. General James Robertson succeeded Tryon as governor.

1781

September 26-28. Prince William Henry, later King William IV, visited New York City.

1783	April 8. The mayor read at City Hall the King's Proclamation which ended the Revolutionary War.

April 17. Governor Robertson sailed for England.

November 25. The British finally evacuated New York City. A great celebration was held. By this time, however, the population of the city had shrunk to 12,000, as many patriots had left the city to escape British domination. |

FROM INDEPENDENCE TO CONSOLIDATION - 1783-1897

1783	December 4. Washington bade farewell to his officers at Fraunces Tavern at Broad and Pearl Streets.
1784	January 21. The New York State Legislature held its first meeting in the City Hall. New York City remained the state capital until 1796, when Albany was chosen to succeed it.

February 5. James Duane was appointed the first mayor after the Revolution.

May 1. King's College was officially changed to Columbia College.

June 9. The first bank in the city opened. It was called the Bank of New York. |
| 1785 | January 11. Congress met in the City Hall (Sub-Treasury Building). New York was named the first capitol of the new United States. It would remain so until 1790. |
| 1786 | The population of the city reached 23,614.

February 14. The first New York City Directory was published.

May. The Tammany Society of New York was organized. Within a few years time, it became a powerful political club led by Aaron Burr.

November 4. The first Roman Catholic Church in the city was opened. It was St. Peter's on Church Street. |
| 1787 | June 15. The first fire insurance company in the city was |

founded. It was the Mutual Assurance Company.

1788   April 13. The so-called Doctor's Riot, lasting two days, occurred. It was caused by popular objection to the practice of dissection. Several persons were killed, and many others injured.

July 23. New Yorkers celebrated the ratification of the new federal Constitution with a spirited parade.

October 6. Repairs and alterations began on City Hall which was to be used by the new Congress. The work was supervised by Charles Pierre L'Enfant, and the building was known as Federal Hall.

1789   March 4. The first Congress under the new Constitution met at Federal Hall.

April 30. George Washington was inaugurated the first president of the United States at Federal Hall.

October 12. Richard Varick succeeded James Duane as mayor.

1790   New York had a population of 33,131.

The old fort at the Battery was torn down. The official residence of the president was erected on this site. It was known as Government House.

March 25. Newly rebuilt Trinity Church opened.

August 12. The final meeting of Congress took place in the city, which ceased being the national capital.

August 30. President Washington left New York.

1791   July. Governor's Island was converted into a recreational area.

August-October. A yellow fever epidemic raged throughout the city. During this epidemic, many residents moved northward to Greenwich Village, thereby helping to develop this suburban area.

1792   The first country club in the city was founded. It was called the Belvedere Club.

	May 17. The New York Stock Exchange had its beginnings when a group of New York brokers formed a brokerage organization.
1794	Bellevue Hospital for Contagious Diseases was opened on the East River.
1795	August-November. Yellow fever again assumed epidemic proportions in New York resulting in several hundred deaths.
1796	The City Hotel opened for business.
	Another yellow fever epidemic struck the city.
	The first black congregation in the city was formed by black members of the Methodist Episcopal Church.
1797	May 1. A second Almshouse was constructed on the north side of the present City Hall Park.
	November 28. The state prison on Washington Street was opened.
1798	Another yellow fever epidemic struck the city.
	January 29. The Park Theater was opened.
1799	April 2. The Manhattan Company was incorporated. It was a private water company whose purpose was to supply the city with an adequate water supply. Its wooden pipe system proved not only inefficient, but also quite unsanitary.
1800	The population of New York was 60,515.
1801	August 24. Edward Livingston succeeded Richard Varick as mayor.
	November 16. The first issue of the <u>New York Evening Post</u> was published.
1802	The Elgin Botanic Garden on Fifth Avenue was established by Dr. David Hosack.
	February 18. A petition to build a bridge across the East River was not acted upon by the Common Council.

1803	May 26. The cornerstone of the present City Hall was laid. Joseph F. Mangin and John McComb Jr. were appointed its architects.

July-November. Yellow fever broke out again in the city causing six hundred deaths. A general suspension of business in the city occurred.

October 29. De Witt Clinton succeeded Edward Livingston as mayor. |
| 1804 | November 20. The New York Historical Society was founded. Its chief organizers were John Pintard and David Hosack. |
| 1805 | February 19. The Free School Society was founded. The public schools of New York City were directed by the Society until 1853. Previous to its organization, the city's schools had been run by charitable, religious, and private organizations. |
| 1806 | Manhattanville was surveyed and laid out as a town.

April 24. The British blockaded New York Harbor in an attempt to stop commercial interchange with the French during the Napoleonic Wars. |
| 1807 | March 16. Marius Willett succeeded De Witt Clinton as mayor.

April 3. Street commissioners were appointed by the Common Council to plan new thoroughfares throughout the upper part of Manhattan Island.

May 2. The first New York guide book <u>The Picture of New York,</u> by Samuel L. Mitchell was published.

August 17. Robert Fulton's steamboat, the <u>Clermont</u> made its first trip from New York to Albany on the Hudson River. |
1808	February 22. De Witt Clinton was again appointed mayor.
1809	February 17. New York's first Sunday newspaper, <u>The Observer</u>, was published. It folded after six months.
1810	The population of New York stood at 96,373.

March 5. Jacob Radcliffe succeeded De Witt Clinton as mayor.

May 1. The first steam ferryboat, the _Raritan_, began making regular trips from the Battery to Perth Amboy, South Amboy, and Elizabethtown.

1811

February 6. De Witt Clinton was appointed mayor for a third time.

August 10. The new City Hall was completed.

August 12. The Common Council held its first regular meeting in the new City Hall.

1812

The first Tammany Hall Building was constructed on Nassau Street. In 1868, Tammany moved to a new building on 14th Street.

May 13. The old City Hall on Wall Street was sold at auction for $425.

June 20. The outbreak of the War of 1812 prompted the Common Council to order new defenses and fortifications.

1813

January 19. New York Harbor was again blockaded by a British fleet. Foreign trade was almost entirely cut off during the spring.

1814

July 6. A British fleet appeared off Sandy Hook. Again, the city government took defensive measures and ordered the construction of several new forts.

October 29. The first steam war vessel, the _Fulton the First_, was launched on the East River. It proved a failure.

1815

February 11. New Yorkers responded to the termination of the War of 1812 with a great celebration. The reopening of American ports to foreign goods brought on an oversupply, resulting in a general business depression for the city during 1816.

March 6. John Ferguson was appointed mayor.

May 6. The first St. Patrick's Cathedral was dedicated.

July 10. Jacob Radcliffe replaced John Ferguson as mayor.

December 25. The Board of Health urged New Yorkers to be vaccinated in order to prevent the spread of smallpox, which began to appear in the city.

1816 January. The Common Council appropriated $1,000 for free vaccinations.

April 12. Brooklyn was incorporated as a village.

May 8. The American Bible Society was organized at City Hall.

1817 The Black Ball Line, from New York to Liverpool was begun. It was the first line of American packet ships to have regular sailing schedules.

1818 February 18. Cadwallader D. Colden was appointed mayor.

1819 March 26. The first savings bank in New York City was chartered by the State Legislature. It was the Bank for Savings.

April. The panic of 1819 struck the city causing severe economic distress.

August 9. The Common Council passed an ordinance prohibiting the use of Velocipedes on sidewalks, and in public places.

September-October. A yellow fever epidemic once again caused the city serious problems. Almost three hundred people died.

1820 New York's population rose to 123,706. It had become the nation's largest city surpassing the old leader, Philadelphia.

1821 March 5. Stephen Allen replaced Colden as mayor.

1822 January 15-17. A new state constitution was approved by the voters of New York State. It was to have a detrimental effect on New York City, because, as the suffrage was extended, corrupt political leaders were given the opportunity to exploit the votes of large blocs of recently arrived immigrants. These characteristics would become fairly commonplace in New York City politics in the future.

1823	March 26. The New York Gaslight Company was chartered.
	May. A franchise for lighting the streets of the city was awarded to the New York Gaslight Company.
1824	The first house in New York City to be lighted with gas was located at 286 Water Street.
	January 19. William Paulding was appointed mayor.
1825	November 4. The Erie Canal was completed. New Yorkers celebrated the event, and in time, the canal brought the city an unmatched prosperity, making it the premier city in America.
	November 29. The first Grand Opera in the United States was produced in New York City at the Park Theater.
1826	January 3. Philip Hone succeeded William Paulding as mayor.
	January 19. The National Academy of Design was founded in New York City.
	December 25. William Paulding was again appointed mayor.
1827	The General Theological Seminary opened.
1828	Washington Square was constructed and opened.
	The National Academy of Design was incorporated.
1829	December 29. Walter Bowne was appointed mayor.
1830	The population of New York was 202,589.
1831	April 18. The University of the City of New York was incorporated.
	November 14. The Richmond Hill Theater was completed and opened.
	December 17. Samuel Ruggles established Gramercy Park by donating the land for its site.
1832	January 28. John Stevens suggested to the Common Council

the construction of an elevated railroad for the city. No action was taken.

July-October. A severe cholera epidemic struck the city. Several thousand residents moved out of the city, thereby helping to settle additional northern suburban areas.

September 18. The Park Theater starred the British music hall favorite, Fanny Kemble.

November 14. The New York and Harlem Railroad opened. It was the first railroad in the city, and its cars were pulled by horses.

1833

Union Square was opened.

The University of the City of New York opened.

January 2. Gideon Lee was appointed mayor.

January 3. Holt's Hotel was opened.

March 3. The City Charter was amended. The amendment gave New Yorkers the right to elect their mayor.

September 3. The New York Sun, a daily, began publication.

October. The first tenement house in the city built specifically for tenement house purposes was constructed.

October 2. William Lloyd Garrison organized the Anti-Slavery Society of New York.

November. Serious riots against abolitionists in the city began.

1834

A serious cholera epidemic took place.

Steam trains were added to the New York and Harlem Railroad.

April 10. The first mayor chosen by popular vote was Cornelius Lawrence.

1835

May 6. The New York Herald first appeared. Its publisher was James Gordon Bennett.

September 23. Parts of Broadway were paved with wooden blocks replacing the macadam surface.

November. Real estate values in the city rose rapidly.

December 16-17. A disastrous fire claimed seven hundred buildings in the heart of the city. It was known as the Great Fire, and it destroyed whatever had remained from Dutch colonial days.

1836   A serious inflationary period struck the city as a result of President Andrew Jackson's removal of federal funds from the Bank of the United States.

February. Living costs skyrocketed sixty-six percent in the city.

March. The Union Club was founded.

May 31. The Astor House Hotel opened.

1837   Samuel F.B. Morse invented the telegraph at his laboratory at New York University.

By the end of 1837, one-sixth of Manhattan Island was urbanized. The rest of it was still occupied by farms and rural surroundings.

February 13. As a result of inflationary prices, a mob of New Yorkers stormed Eli Hart's flour warehouse, helping themselves to large amounts of flour, and destroying bushels of wheat and flour barrels.

March. Several food warehouses were looted by irate New Yorkers.

The panic of 1837 began. It caused serious troubles for New York.

April 8. Ninety-eight businesses went bankrupt as a result of the panic, and a run on all banks occurred.

April 11. Aaron Clark was elected mayor.

1838   April 22. The first fully steam-powered vessel to reach New York, the *Sirius*, arrived from Europe.

April 23. A second fully-steam-powered vessel, the Great Western, arrived from Europe.

August. The Halls of Justice in the Tombs were completed.

1839   An express service from New York to Boston was established by William F. Harriden.

Construction began on High Bridge across the Harlem River. This bridge was a link in the Croton Aqueduct System.

April 9. Isaac L. Varian was elected mayor.

1840   The population of the city stood at 312,710.

May 14. The famous European dancer, Fanny Ellsler, starred at the Park Theater.

1841   The Manual of the Common Council was published under the editorship of David T. Valentine, who held the post for twenty-five years.

April 10. The first issue of the New York Tribune appeared. Its publisher was Horace Greeley.

April 13. Robert H. Morris was elected mayor.

1842   The Griscom Report, concerned with the health of the city, was written by the city inspector, John H. Griscom.

February 14. Charles Dickens visited New York.

April 11. A Board of Education was appointed. It consisted of five trustees, two inspectors, and two commissioners, who would supervise the ward schools. These men were to be elected in each of the wards.

July 4. The first water from the Croton Aqueduct System was brought to the central reservoir on 5th Avenue at 42nd Street.

October 14. The Croton Aqueduct System was finally completed at a cost of $12,500,000. Charles King was the architect in charge.

1843   The first ward school opened.

The Association for Improving the Condition of the Poor was founded.

1844   April 9. James Harper was elected mayor.

May 7. A new police force of eight hundred men was enacted for the city by the State Legislature.

1845   April 8. William F. Havemeyer was elected mayor.

May. The first contingents of new city policemen began appearing on the streets.

July 19. A serious fire again burned the downtown district causing severe damages.

September 3. The Knickerbocker Baseball Club was founded.

1846   An electric telegraph line between New York and Philadelphia began operating.

April 14. Andrew H. Mickle was elected mayor.

May 20. New Yorkers approved the Declaration of War against Mexico in a rally held in City Hall Park.

May 21. The present Trinity Church at Wall Street was dedicated.

Madison Square was opened.

April 13. William V. Brady was elected mayor.

May 7. The Board of Education was permitted by the State Legislature to open the Free Academy.

1848   The Five Points Mission and House of Industry was organized. The driving force behind its establishment was the New York Ladies' Home Missionary Society.

April 11. William F. Havemeyer was elected mayor for a second time.

1849   The Brooklyn City Hall was opened.

January. The Free Academy opened.

January 18. The Astor Library was incorporated. John Jacob Astor donated the money for its establishment.

April 2. The City Charter was amended. Nine executive departments were created, and the mayor's term was increased to two years.

April 10. Caleb S. Woodhull was elected mayor.

May 7-10. Rivalry between two actors, Edwin Forrest, and William Macready, produced the Astor Place Riots, during which nearly two hundred persons were killed or injured.

May-June. A serious cholera epidemic again struck the city.

1850   The population of New York reached 515,394. Another 150,000 lived in the suburbs.

August 2. Guiseppi Garibaldi arrived in New York.

September 11. P.T. Barnum brought the "Swedish Nightingale," Jenny Lind to New York, where she gave her first concert at Castle Garden.

November 5. Ambrose C. Kingsland was elected mayor.

1851   September 18. The New York Times was first published.

December 6. Louis Kossuth, the Hungarian revolutionary, arrived in New York.

1852   June 30. The first Y.M.C.A. in the United States was opened in New York.

November 2. Jacob A. Westervelt was elected mayor.

1853   May 2. Franconi's Hippodrome was opened.

June 30. The Latting Observatory was opened.

July 14. The first American World's Fair was held at the Crystal Palace in New York.

1854   November 7. Fernando Wood was elected mayor. He can be considered the first of a long line of corrupt public officials in the city.

1855	The Workingmen's Home Association constructed a model tenement.
	May 17. Mt. Sinai Hospital, originally called the Jews Hospital, was opened.
	August 3. Castle Garden was converted into an immigrant depot.
1857	Frederick L. Olmsted and Calvert Vaux, landscape architects, began construction of Central Park
	June 16. A pitched battle occurred at City Hall between Fernando Wood's Municipal Police Force, and the State Legislature's newly created Metropolitan Police Force. It took an army regiment to quell the riot.
	July 4-5. A gang feud between the Bowery Boys and the Dead Rabbits erupted into two days of rioting.
	August 24. The panic of 1857 began. New Yorkers again suffered hard times, but recovery was more rapid than twenty years earlier.
	December 1. Daniel F. Tiemann was elected mayor.
1858	May 11. St. Luke's Hospital was opened.
	August 15. The cornerstone of the present St. Patrick's Cathedral was laid.
	August 18. A fire broke out in City Hall destroying the upper floor and part of the roof.
	November 24. Fernando Wood was elected mayor in a very corrupt-ridden election.
1860	The population of New York reached 814,000.
	February 27. Abraham Lincoln gave his famous Cooper Union speech.
	June 14. The first issue of the <u>New York World</u> appeared.
1861	The County Court House in City Hall Park was begun.

CHRONOLOGY

April 12. The start of the Civil War caused most New Yorkers to support Lincoln and the Union cause.

April 19. The Seventh Regiment of New York Volunteers left for the battlefield.

April 20. A huge rally was held in Union Square, where New Yorkers pledged their loyalty to the government.

December 3. George Opdyke was elected mayor.

1862   January 30. The steel ship *Monitor* was launched at Greenpoint.

July 1. When news of General George B. McClellan's defeat on the peninsula became known in the city, a mild panic occurred on Wall Street.

1863   February 6. New York Republicans established the Union League Club.

July 13-16. Serious draft riots occurred in the city. About one thousand persons were killed or injured, and property damage stood at about one million dollars.

December 1. C. Godfrey Gunther was elected mayor.

1864   April 4. The Metropolitan Fair opened. Its purpose was to raise money for the Union cause, and it took in over a million dollars.

November 25. Several Southern spies unsuccessfully attempted to set fire to New York.

1865   March 30. A Metropolitan Fire District, and a New York Fire Department were established. The volunteeer fire companies were disbanded.

April 10. Robert E. Lee's surrender at Appomattox evoked great rejoicing in the city.

April 12. New Yorkers were profoundly saddened by the assassination of Abraham Lincoln.

April 24. President Lincoln's body lay in state at City Hall, and was viewed by some 120,000 people.

April 28. The University Club was incorporated.

November 13. The Manhattan Club was founded.

December 5. John T. Hoffman was elected mayor.

1866　　The Free Academy was changed to the College of the City of New York.

February 26. A Board of Health, and a Metropolitan Sanitary District were created by the State Legislature.

1867　　April 11. A United States Post Office Building was built at the lower end of City Hall Park.

May 14. The first New York Tenement House Law was enacted.

December 7. Charles Dickens visited New York for a second time.

1868　　July 3. An elevated railroad was begun on Ninth Avenue by Charles Harvey.

July 4. The Democratic National Convention met at Tammany Hall.

November 30. Mayor Hoffman resigned. The President of the Board of Aldermen, Thomas Coman, became mayor.

1869　　The first modern apartment house in New York opened. It was called the Stuyvesant.

April 6. The American Museum of Natural History was incorporated.

September 24. The infamous Black Friday occurred in the city when Jay Gould, James Fisk, and other financiers tried to corner the gold supply on Wall Street.

November 23. The Metropolitan Museum of Art was established.

December. A Normal School for the training of teachers was set up by the Board of Education.

December 1. A. Oakey Hall was elected mayor.

1870

The population of the city stood at 942,292.

The city's Normal School was opened.

The Association of the Bar of New York City was founded.

February 26. The first subway in the city was opened by the Beach Pneumatic Transit Company. It ran in a tunnel under Broadway, but because of public objections, it was closed down.

April 5. The State Legislature approved a new charter for the city. This was the notorious Tweed Charter which gave Boss Tweed virtual control over New York.

1871

The Knickerbocker Club was founded.

January 14. Thomas Nast's devastating cartoons, exposing the corruption of the Tweed Ring, appeared in Harper's Weekly.

February. George Jones, editor of the New York Times, began an editorial attack on the Tweed Ring.

April 6. A great mass meeting was held at Cooper Institute to raise protest against the passage by the State Legislature of a number of bills sponsored by Boss Tweed.

September 4. Another mass meeting took place at Cooper Institute chaired by ex-Mayor William F. Havemeyer. A Committee of Seventy was chosen to oppose the Tweed Ring, and to institute reforms in city government.

October 9. The first Grand Central Station was opened.

November 3. Tweed Ring candidates were defeated for city offices.

1872

October 10. The Presbyterian Hospital was incorporated and opened.

November 5. William F. Havemeyer was elected mayor for a third time.

1873	April 30. The city received a new charter. It revised many of the clauses of the Tweed Charter.
	May 23. The towns of Kingsbridge, West Farms, and Morrisania were annexed to the city.
	September 18. The panic of 1873 began. New York was again hard hit.
1874	November 3. William H. Wickham was elected mayor.
	November 30. Mayor Havemeyer died in office. Samuel B. Vance, president of the Board of Aldermen, became acting mayor.
1876	November 7. Smith Ely was elected mayor.
1877	The American Museum of Natural History moved to its present site.
	The Lenox Library was opened.
1878	June 5. An elevated railway on Sixth Avenue was opened.
	August 26. The Third Avenue Elevated Railway was opened.
	Private citizens opened the New York Free Circulating Library.
	In a competition sponsored by the magazine <u>Sanitary Engineer</u>, James E. Ware's design for the "dumbbell" tenement won first prize. It became the prototype for tenements that now mushroomed all over the city.
	March. The Bell Telephone Company opened the first telephone exchange in the city.
	June 16. An amendment was added to the Tenement House Law of 1867. Its purpose was to improve tenement house conditions in the city.
1880	The population of the city reached 1,164,673.
	The Metropolitan Museum of Art moved to its present site.
	November 2. William R. Grace was elected mayor.

November 8. Sarah Bernhardt made her American debut at Booth's Theater in New York.

December 20. Brush electric arc lamps were installed on Broadway.

1881 February 22. The Egyptian government gave an obelisk to the United States. It was given to New York City by the federal government and placed on a pedestal in Central Park. The obelisk is known as Cleopatra's Needle.

May 26. The statue of Admiral Farragut was unveiled in Madison Square.

1882 September 4. Thomas Edison's huge dynamos were turned on, and several sections of the city glowed with electric light for the first time.

November 6. Lily Langtry appeared at Wallach's Tehater for the first time.

November 7. Franklin Edison was elected mayor.

1883 May 24. Brooklyn Bridge was opened. It was the first bridge across the East River.

October 22. The Metropolitan Opera House was opened.

1884 June 14. By act of the State Legislature, all telephone, telegraph, and electric wires were to be removed from the city's streets.

July 14. Sites were acquired by the city government for the establishment of a number of parks in the Bronx.

August 30. A fraudulent franchise was granted to the Broadway Surface Railroad Company by the Board of Aldermen.

1886 Two years after a franchise had been awarded to the Broadway Surface Railroad Company, investigation revealed gross irregularities and corruption.

October 28. The Statue of Liberty was unveiled in New York Harbor. Its sculptor-engineer was Frederic Bartholdi. The statue was a gift of the French people to the American people.

November 2. Abram S. Hewitt was elected mayor.

1888   One of the earliest examples of steel skeleton construction was the Tower Building.

January 9. The Reform Club was founded.

March 11-14. The city was paralyzed by the Great Blizzard of '88.

November 6. Hugh J. Grant was elected mayor.

1889   October 7. Barnard College opened.

November. The World Building was erected.

1890   The population of New York City reached 1,441,216.

June 16. Madison Square Garden opened.

1891   April 28. A botanical garden was opened in Bronx Park.

June 24. The new Croton Aqueduct, with a capacity of 300,000,000 gallons daily, was completed after eight years of work.

1892   The Metropolitan Opera House burned to the ground.

January 1. Ellis Island was converted into the city's immigrant depot.

October 12. The Columbus Monument at Columbus Circle was dedicated.

November 8. Thomas G. Gilroy was elected mayor.

December 27. The cornerstone of the Cathedral of St. John the Divine was laid.

1893   The Metropolitan Life Insurance Building was begun.

March 14. The Waldorf Hotel was opened.

1894   January 31. The Lexow Committee was appointed to investigate the activities of the New York Police Department. The committee uncovered connections between the police and certain aspects of organized crime. As a result, a number of indictments and convictions were obtained.

November 6. William L. Strong was elected mayor.

1895   January 17. Richard W. Gilder chaired a third Tenement House Commission.

May 4. The Washington Arch in Washington Square Park was completed. Its architect was Stanford White.

May 23. The New York Public Library was formed when the Astor Library, Lenox Library, and the Tilden Trust combined their separate library corporations.

June 6. The city annexed the towns of Wakefield, Williamsbridge, Eastchester, and parts of Pelham and Westchester.

1896.   Ernest Flagg won first prize for a new tenement house design. The contest was sponsored by the Improved Housing Council.

December 10. An aquarium was opened in Castle Garden.

1897   February 22. The Citizen's Union was formed.

April 27. Grant's Tomb was dedicated and opened by President William McKinley.

May 4. The five boroughs were consolidated into one city by the terms of the Greater New York Charter. The charter went into effect on January 1, 1898. Consolidation increased the city's population to 3,100,000 and its area to 359 square miles.

September 13. The first public high schools in the city were opened. They were DeWitt Clinton, Morris, and Wadley.

November 2. Robert A. Van Wyck was elected the first mayor of Greater New York.

December. The Waldorf-Astoria Hotel was opened.

1898-1939 GREATER NEW YORK

1898   January 1. The Consolidation Act of 1897 officially began to operate, uniting Manhattan, Brooklyn, Queens, the Bronx, and Staten Island as one municipality.

1899   March 17. The Hotel Windsor was burned to the ground.

October 23. The Third Avenue surface line introduced electric-powered cars. Electricity soon was being used for all means of transportation.

1900   The population of New York City stood at 3,437,202.

November 3. An automobile show was held at Madison Square Garden.

1901   March 12. A gift of sixty-five branch libraries was given to the city by Andrew Carnegie.

April 22. Several important amendments were added to the Greater New York Charter.

November 5. Seth Low was elected mayor.

1902   The tallest building in New York, the Flatiron Building was constructed.

May 30. The Soldiers' and Sailors' monument on Riverside Drive was dedicated.

1903   November 2. George B. McClellan was elected mayor.

December 19. The Williamsburgh Bridge was opened.

1904   March 11. The first of the tubes under the Hudson River between New York and Jersey City was completed.

October 27. The West Side Subway was opened to the public. It ran from City Hall to West 145th Street.

1905   All of the tubes under the Hudson River to New Jersey were completed.

1906   The 69th Regiment Armory was constructed.

October 9. The Pennsylvania Railroad tunnels under the Hudson River were completed.

CHRONOLOGY 39

1907   January. A report was delivered to Mayor McClellan by the New York City Improvement Commission, which recommended the development of uniformly constructed piers along the Hudson River, as well as other civic improvements.

July 30. Motor buses replaced all horse-drawn public vehicles in the city.

October 1. New taxicabs appeared in New York. Each cab contained a meter to determine the fare.

1908   March 18. The Pennsylvania Railroad tunnels under the East River were completed.

May 1. The Singer Building was constructed.

May 14. The College of the City opened its first five buildings.

1909   June 12. The Queensborough Bridge was opened.

June 16. A State Committee, appointed by Governor Charles Evans Hughes to investigate the activities of Wall Street banks and brokerage houses, recommended stringent legislation to regulate the various exchanges.

July 1. Police Commissioner R. Bingham was removed from office by Mayor McClellan for insubordination.

September 29. Wilbur Wright made the first airplane flight over the city.

November 3. William J. Gaynor was elected mayor.

December 31. The Manhattan Bridge was completed.

1910   The population of Greater New York stood at 4,746,883.

August 9. A deranged ex-city worker unsuccessfully attempted to assassinate Mayor Gaynor. John Purroy Mitchell, president of the Board of Aldermen, served as acting mayor during Gaynor's recovery period.

September 8. Pennsylvania Railroad Station was opened.

1911	March. The Tenement House Acts were attacked as inadequate by the New York Commission on Congestion of Population.
1912	The Brooklyn Public Central Library Building at Grand Army Plaza was constructed.
	July 16. The sensational Becker Trial took place. It again involved connections between New York Police and criminal elements.
1913	Bronx County was created.
	The Woolworth Building was constructed. Cass Gilbert was the architect in charge.
	March 19. The so-called dual system of subways and elevated railways was created by the city government when it signed contracts with the Interborough Rapid Transit Company and the New York Municipal Railway Company.
	September 10. Mayor Gaynor died. Once again, John Purroy Mitchell served as acting mayor.
	November 4. John Purroy Mitchell was elected mayor.
1914	The present day Municipal Building was constructed.
	The present day General Post Office was constructed.
	March 27. The tercentenary of the New Netherland Company was observed.
	April 17. Mayor Mitchell escaped unharmed from an assassination attempt. Corporation Counsel Frank L. Polk, however, was wounded.
	August 28. The outbreak of World War I in Europe was greeted with mixed emotions by most New Yorkers.
1915	January 6. Two people were killed, and one hundred and seventy-two injured in an accident on the I.R.T. subway.
1916	January 3-July 1. The Thompson Legislative Investigating Committee revealed instances of corruption and graft involving subway construction company officials.
	July. Poliomyelitis struck the city causing 2,362 deaths.

July 22. Trolley car operators went on strike, closing down most urban surface transportation.

July 25. The Common Council adopted New York City's first zoning ordinance.

1917	April 6. The United States entered World War I. New Yorkers wholeheartedly supported the government's decision.

April 27. The 27th Division, New York National Guard, left for training camps. It was the first, but certainly not the last, of the military units from New York City to go to war.

November 6. John F. Hylan was elected mayor. |
| 1918 | August-December. A serious epidemic of Spanish Influenza raged throughout the city.

November 11. New Yorkers welcomed the armistice ending World War I. During the war, the city served as one of the major ports of embarkation for American troops going overseas. More than 1,500,000 men left for Europe from New York's piers. |
| 1919 | Fourteen new piers were constructed on Staten Island. |
| 1920 | The population of the city reached 5,620,048. |
| 1921 | April 30. The New York Port Authority was created.

October 28. Marshal Ferdinand Foch visited the city.

November 8. John F. Hylan was re-elected mayor. |
1922	November 17. The French Premier, Georges Clemenceau, visited New York.
1923	The Museum of the City of New York was founded.
1924	November 3. James J. Walker was elected mayor.
1925	The Welfare Council of the City of New York was founded.
1926	November 17-19. New York celebrated its tercentenary.

1927	June 11. A great ticker-tape parade was held for Charles A. Lindbergh on his return to New York after his solo flight to France.
	November 11. The Holland Tunnel was completed and opened.
1928	June 20. The Goethals Bridge and the Outerbridge Crossing from Staten Island to New Jersey were opened to the public.
1929	April 19. The old Tenement House Acts were replaced by the passage of a new Multiple Dwelling Law.
	May 27. The Regional Plan Association of New York submitted its report calling for a series of improvements in the city.
	June. Jones Beach State Park was opened to the public.
	October 29. The stock market crash on Wall Street ushered in a nationwide depression, which lasted deep into the 1930's.
	November 5. James J. Walker was re-elected mayor.
1930	The population of New York City reached 6,930,446.
	The Chrysler Building was completed. It was seventy-seven stories high.
	November 13. The first part of the West Side Highway was opened to vehicular traffic.
	December 11. As the depression deepened, bank failures in New York mounted. The Bank of the United States, one of the largest in the nation, closed its doors.
1931	Then the tallest building in the world, the Empire State Building (102 stories) was completed.
	The new Waldorf-Astoria Hotel was opened.
	February 26. The <u>New York World-Telegram</u> was first published.
	March 24. Judge Samuel Seabury headed an investigation

into New York City government. The Seabury Committee uncovered flagrant abuses in City Hall, leading to the removal of a number of city officials including the Sheriff of New York County, Thomas M. (Tin Box Tom) Farley.

October 24. The George Washington Bridge, which crossed the Hudson River to New Jersey, was completed and opened. It was the longest suspension bridge in the world.

November 14. The Bayonne Bridge from Staten Island to New Jersey was completed and opened.

1932 New York Hospital-Cornell Medical School was opened.

Rockefeller Center's first two buildings were completed.

April 10. By this date 828,000 New Yorkers were receiving charity from public and private sources.

April 29. Some $5,000,000 was appropriated by the Board of Estimate for the relief of unemployed New Yorkers, and an additional $1,000,000 was voted for veterans' relief.

September 1. Mayor Walker resigned as a result of the Seabury Committee's revelations. Joseph V. McKee, president of the Board of Aldermen, became acting mayor.

September 10. The Independent Subway System, wholly city owned, was completed and opened.

November 8. John P. O'Brien was elected mayor to complete the rest of Mayor Walker's term.

1933 March 4. President Franklin D. Roosevelt closed all banks in the country including those in New York.

November 7. Fiorello H. LaGuardia was elected mayor.

1934 The federal government took over the operations of Wall Street during the economic emergency.

By means of an R.F.C. loan, a new housing project, Knickerbocker Village, was constructed.

December 11. The city government enacted a two percent sales tax to be used for unemployment relief.

1935	January 13. A Charter Commission headed by Thomas D. Thacher was appointed by Mayor LaGuardia to draft a new charter for the city.

July 29. A special investigation of crime in the city was undertaken by Thomas E. Dewey, who was appointed prosecutor by Governor Herbert Lehman.

October 3. The Hayden Planetarium was opened to the public.

October 12. Fort Tryon Park was dedicated and opened to the public. |
| 1936 | Buses began to replace trolley cars on city streets.

January 19. The Theodore Roosevelt Memorial was unveiled.

February 7. The City Penitentiary on Welfare Island was shut down. The prison on Rikers Island replaced it.

March. Construction began on the Sixth Avenue subway.

July 11. The Triborough Bridge across the East River was completed.

October 2. Construction began on the Queens-Midtown Tunnel.

November 3. The new City Charter was approved by New York voters.

December 12. Construction was completed on the Henry Hudson Bridge over Spuyten Duyvil Creek. |
| 1937 | The Harlem River Houses, and the Williamsburg Homes, two P.W.A. housing complexes were completed.

The first section of the East River Drive was completed.

The Citizen's Housing Council of New York was formed.

October 12. Construction was completed on the Henry Hudson Parkway. |

November 2. Fiorello H. LaGuardia was re-elected mayor. At the same time, Thomas E. Dewey was chosen District Attorney for Manhattan, and the first new City Council was selected by the voters.

December 21. The Lincoln Tunnel's first two tubes were completed.

1938   The population of the city had grown to 7,505,068.

The Greater New York Fund was founded.

January 1. The so-called La Guardia Charter officially went into operation.

October 17. Governor Lehman appointed John Harlan Amen special prosecutor to look into corruption in Brooklyn.

December 5. The Sixth Avenue El was torn down.

1939   Construction was completed on the Bronx-Whitestone Bridge.

April 1. The Association for Improving the Condition of the Poor, and the Charity Organization Society merged as the Community Service Society of New York.

April 30. The New York World's Fair was opened by President Roosevelt, Governor Lehman, and Mayor LaGuardia. The Fair, at Flushing Meadows, Queens, lasted for a year.

1940-1970   THE SUPER CITY

1940   The population of the city was 7,454,995, a slight decrease as compared with preceding years. This was caused by a movement to the suburbs.

The city assumed the management of a unified subway system by purchasing the privately owned B.M.T. and I.R.T. systems, and combining them with the city built and owned Independent Subway System.

February 21. The Sub-Treasury Building on Wall Street became a national monument, Federal Hall Memorial.

1941   Mayor LaGuardia initiated work on the mammoth air terminal in the Idlewild district in Queens, now known as John F. Kennedy Memorial Airport.

The work of various independent city agencies was made part of the larger Central Welfare Agency.

November 4. Fiorello H. LaGuardia was elected mayor for a third time.

December 7. New York City reacted to the outbreak of World War II with a sort of "grim acceptance of inevitability."

1942 January 1. Broadway, the Great White Way, had its electric lights extinguished, and all windows above the tenth floor blacked out.

1944 February. The new construction program to draw water from the Delaware River for the city water supply, begun in 1936, was half completed. In 1955, the second half of the project was finished.

1945 The city's transit facilities comprised 554 miles of route, and 1,237 miles of track. The subway was serving 7,750,000 persons per day.

April 1. By this date, nearly 900,000 New Yorkers had been inducted into the armed forces.

May 8. Despite the scarcity of paper, ticker tape rained on Broadway following news of the German surrender in May, and again in August with the news of the Japanese capitulation.

November 4. William O'Dwyer, a Democrat, was elected mayor, when LaGuardia stepped down because of ill health.

1946 The United Nations settled in New York City in its permanent headquarters on seventeen acres of land donated to the international body by the Rockefeller family. The buildings of the United Nations were constructed between 1949 and 1954.

September. Mayor O'Dwyer instituted a far reaching program of administrative reforms, creating the division of Analysis in the Bureau of the Budget.

1947	April 15. The Jewish Museum, first of its kind in the United States, located in the former home of Felix Warburg, opened.

September 20. Fiorello H. LaGuardia died.

October. New York City accepted the principle of refusing to deal with the so-called Communist Unions.

November 3. The old twenty-five member City Council, elected by a system of proportional representation, was abolished by popular referendum. Councilmen were now to be elected by a simple majority vote. |
| 1948 | July 1. A ten cent fare for the transit system was adopted. It was the first increase in fares since the system began. |
| 1949 | The Brooklyn Battery Tunnel was opened to vehicular traffic.

June. The city administration accepted collective bargaining with the subway unions.

October 25. President Harry S Truman came to New York to lay the cornerstone of the first building to be constructed at United Nations Plaza.

November 8. William O'Dwyer was re-elected mayor. |
| 1950 | The population of the city stood at 7,891,957. There were 750,000 blacks, and 325,000 Puerto Ricans residing in New York. The Census reported that fifty-six percent of New York City's residents were foreign born or of foreign or mixed parentage.

September 1. William O'Dwyer resigned as mayor, after disclosures of scandal and fraud in his administration.

November 6. Vincent R. Impelliteri, a Democrat running on the Independent Experience Party, defeated Tammany candidate, Ferdinand Pecora, for the mayoralty in a special election. |
| 1951 | November 17. The first attempt at a comprehensive revision of the city's zoning law failed to be enacted by the City Council. |

1953	The Puerto Rican born population of the city was 469,000. By 1955, the number had dropped to 380,000 because many Puerto Ricans returned home.
	November 3. Robert F. Wagner defeated Rudolph Halley, and Harold Riegelmann for the mayoralty.
1955	June 1. New York City's subway and bus system was put under the professional management of a Transit Authority.
	September. The Third Avenue Elevated Railroad was demolished. It had been the city's oldest elevated rapid transit line.
	October. The city administration instituted a massive drive against litter, and in 1958, violations began to be issued to "litter bugs."
1956	March 8. New York City opened its first heliport on West 30th Street. It was run by the New York Port Authority.
	September. The City Planning Commission embarked upon an attempt to revise the city's zoning laws. In 1960, the Commission's proposals were accepted, and by 1965 the new regulations were in effect.
1957	The population of the city was 7,795,471, a slight decrease from the 1950 Census figure.
	March. A third tube was added to the Lincoln Tunnel, the only triple underwater tunnel in the world.
	April. The New York Standard Metropolitan Area (S.M.A.) totaled 12,911,994 residents.
	November 5. Robert F. Wagner was re-elected mayor, defeating Robert K. Christenberry, the Republican candidate.
1958	Mayor Wagner proposed the creation of a charter revision committee, but the measure was not passed by the Council.
	June 10. The New York City Health Research Council was created.
1959	The assessed value of real estate in New York City stood at $32,000,000,000, while the value of taxable property was

set at just under $22,500,000,000. By 1964, it had grown to over $28,500,000,000.

May 5. The city Board of Health enacted a new health code that replaced the old Sanitary Code.

September 18. A one day work-stoppage by members of the State, County, and Municipal Employees Union took place.

1960

The West Side Urban Renewal Project, encompassing a massive urban renewal program, was begun. It has continued to the present.

January 14. Manhattan Borough President, Hulan Jack, was indicted for conspiracy to obstruct justice and for three violations of the City Charter.

February. A New York State Commission on Governmental Operations of the city of New York was highly critical of the city administration, which it charged, was inefficient, corrupt, and graft-ridden.

March 26. Mayor Wagner and Governor Nelson Rockefeller reached an agreement whereby, the city would gain substantial state aid as a result of a new fiscal program.

June 29. Bedloe's Island, the site of the Statue of Liberty, had its name changed to Liberty Island.

September 10. New York City public school teachers went out on strike.

October 1. Robert Moses, City Construction Coordinator, and Commissioner of Parks, resigned his positions to assume the presidency of the World's Fair Corporation.

November. A new Housing and Redevelopment Board took over the work of the old Committee on Slum Clearance, the Urban Renewal Board, and the Neighborhood Conservation Unit.

December. The creation of the City University of New York was proposed. This plan united all the four year colleges and community colleges of the city under one Board of Higher Education. The plan began to operate during the following year.

1961   The Throgs Neck Bridge connecting the Bronx with Queens was opened to vehicular traffic.

The complicated arrangements to help improve the New York commuter services of the Long Island, New Haven, and New York Central Railroads were completed.

June 6. Robert F. Wagner defeated Arthur Levitt, the state comptroller in the Democratic mayoral primary. Wagner opposed Tammany leaders including Carmine De Sapio of Manhattan, who backed Levitt.

September. A spectacular reconstitution of the Board of Education took place following disclosures of irregularities in the contracting practices of the school system.

November 8. Wagner defeated Republican candidate Louis J. Lefkowitz for mayor.

The voters of New York approved a revision of the 1936 charter, which changed a number of structural and procedural features of the city government.

December 3. Mayor Wagner demanded the resignations of four hundred employees in top city jobs, in a move to spur the ouster of those who owed their positions to the Democratic bosses.

1962   The lower level of the George Washington Bridge was opened.

The antidiscriminatory authority of the Commission on Human Relations was strengthened by new provisions of the Fair Housing Practices Act, and a Rent and Rehabilitation Administration was created.

The city government seized the Fifth Avenue Coach Company, and established a special authority to operate it.

January. Approval was granted by the Legislatures of New York and New Jersey for the construction of the World Trade Center under the control of the Port Authority.

September. Mayor Wagner named a panel of twenty-five distinguished lawyers and civic leaders to review the qualifications of nominees for judicial offices.

New York City teachers conducted a one day work stoppage to achieve better working conditions.

1963

The Lincoln Center Cultural and Art complex was begun.

May 1. Although there was considerable opposition, the City Council raised the general sales tax from three to four percent, as well as enacting a number of other city taxes.

July 1. A precedent was broken when Dr. Calvin Gross was appointed superintendent of schools. Gross, from Pittsburgh, was the first non-New Yorker ever appointed to head this department.

August. A new Department of Relocation, reporting directly to the mayor, was created, and members were appointed.

1964

The two-deck Verrazano-Narrows Bridge, with a span of 4,260 feet, opened between Brooklyn and Staten Island.

April 5. The New York World's Fair built at Flushing Meadows, Queens, was opened. It ran for almost two years.

June 6. Charles A. Buckley, old time Democratic boss of the Bronx, lost the nomination for Congress to reform Democrat, Jonathan B. Bingham, in a bitter primary.

July. A major race riot took place in Harlem, touched off by the killing of a young black boy.

1965

New York City had the largest factory work force of any American city with nearly a million industrial workers, and the largest manufacturing payroll, close to three billion dollars a year.

By 1965, Mayor Wagner had substantially reformed the Democratic party. His reform organization defeated Tammany chief, Carmine DeSapio, in DeSapio's own assembly district.

The expense budget of the city stood at $3.4 billion.

January. The Board of Education forced the resignation of its superintendent, Dr. Calvin Gross.

April 21. New York City social workers went out on strike.

November. As a result of the United States Supreme Court's decision in 1962, concerning state legislative districts and reapportionment, there was a substantial increase in the city's representation in Albany.

November 5. John V. Lindsay, a Republican, was elected mayor.

November 9. New York City was hit very hard by a power failure which blacked out the northeastern United States. Some sections of the city had no electricity for thirteen hours or more.

1966 New York City experienced a severe area drought, with an accompanying water shortage that caused the city government to enact special regulations concerning the use of water.

July. Another race riot broke out in the east New York section of Brooklyn; however, it was not as violent as the riot two years earlier.

July 1. A tax reform program began in New York City, which included a commuter income tax and a city income tax.

September. Parent demonstrations took place in Harlem against a new $5,000,000 school (P.S. 201) because the student body was de facto all black.

1967 January 4. Adam Clayton Powell, popular black Congressman from Harlem, was barred from Congress for misusing public funds. Despite these facts, his Harlem constituency re-elected him.

April 15. Mayor Lindsay formed the Summer Task Force in an effort to avoid potential trouble during the coming summer.

July. Rioting and antipolice disorders broke out in East Harlem and in the Puerto Rican slums in the Bronx.

September 7. The City Council created the Urban Action Task Force on a year round basis.

1968 Construction on the Port Authority's twin one hundred and ten story towers for the World Trade Center in lower Manhattan was begun.

The fourth Madison Square Garden, built over Pennsylvania Station, was formally opened.

A bitter teachers strike took place; the police were engaged in work slowdowns; the firemen and sanitation men were threatening similar job actions, and a flu epidemic struck the city with full force.

April 4. Only minor rioting broke out in New York City as a result of the assassination of Martin Luther King.

April 23. Students for a Democratic Society (SDS), at Columbia University, led a violent demonstration to protest the University's proposed construction of a new gymnasium on the site of a park in Harlem. Other major demonstrations took place throughout the year at almost all of the city's institutions of higher learning.

April 26. A giant antiwar rally took place in New York. Two hundred thousand students in the New York metropolitan area cut classes to participate in the marches and demonstrations, culminating in an 87,000 person rally in Central Park's Sheep Meadow.

May. A dispute in the predominately black Ocean-Hill-Brownsville section in Brooklyn between an experimental, neighborhood-run public school district, and a group of union teachers in that district, precipitated the teachers' strike.

October 15. A great Vietnam War Moratorium was held in New York City, as well as across the nation.

1969

February. The worst snow storm in twenty-five years struck the city, and hit with particular force in eastern Queens.

October. The New York Mets professional baseball team won the World Series. They had been formed seven years earlier.

November 4. John V. Lindsay was re-elected mayor. He had been defeated in the Republican primary by State Senator John Marchi, but put together a coalition of liberals from from both parties, and won the election over Marchi and Democrat Abraham Beame.

1970

The Census reported New York City's population was 7,957,341, while the New York Standard Metropolitan Area totaled more the 13,500,000.

In 1970, the Census reported that 1,200,000 residents or fifteen percent of the city's population lived in poverty.

January. New York City, with the cooperation of the New York Telephone Company, instituted the first three-digit emergency phone number in the country (911).

January 1. Bus and subway fares were increased by fifty percent.

May 9. Helmeted construction workers broke up an anti-Vietnam, student demonstration, and chased the students through the downtown financial district.

May 13. Mayor Lindsay announced the formation of the Mayor's Council on the Environment.

May 22. Mayor Lindsay appointed a special commission to investigate police corruption. Headed by Whitman Knapp, its was known and the Knapp Commission.

June 13. An area in Brownsville, designated for the Model Cities Program, was the scene of rioting and violence as a result of huge accumulations of garbage that had not been removed by the Sanitation Department.

July 5. Howard Samuels was appointed chairman of the Off-Track Betting Corporation of the city.

July 17. A Vermont educator, Harvey Scribner, was named the new chancellor of the troubled New York City school system.

September 12. Patrick V. Murphy was appointed the new police commissioner.

September 14. The City University of New York began an open admissions policy, which allowed all students who graduated from the city high schools to participate in some form of higher education.

November 18. Mayor Lindsay ordered the layoff of five hundred provisional employees to ease the budget crisis. It was the first mass action of this sort since the depression.

November. Community control of local school districts went into effect throughout the city.

DOCUMENTS

The documents that follow are only a small sampling of the vast amount of primary materials available to the student interested in doing research on the history and development of New York City. Practically all of the documents relating to New York City can be found in volumes of secondary works. These are readily available at most of the central public libraries throughout the city. The New York Public Library and the New-York Historical Society Library have especially fine collections, but much material can also be found at the library of the Museum of the City of New York, and at the Municipal Library, which houses a huge collection of public documents. Some of the original documents are in the special collections of the New York Public Library, and a few can be found at the New-York Historical Society. Both Columbia University and New York University are repositories of both public and private documents and papers in their original form. The greatest problem one encounters when compiling documents concerned with New York City is selectivity. There is such an abundance of materials that wading through them becomes an almost impossible task. However, the documents section of this volume attempts to give the reader as varied a selection of documents as possible within the confines of a small book. Space limitations aside, the documents included here provide, like the other sections of this work, an excellent starting point for further research into a complex and fascinating area of historical study.

THE CHARTER OF FREEDOMS AND EXEMPTIONS - 1629

In order to promote colonization to New Netherlands, the Dutch West India Company issued a Charter of Freedoms and Exemptions. Part of the Charter follows.

(Source: E.B. O'Callaghan, <u>Documents Relative to the Colonial History of the State of New York</u>, II, Albany, 1856.)

All such shall be acknowledged Patroons of New Netherland who shall, within the space of four years next after they have given notice to any of the Chambers of the Company here, or to the Commander or Council there, undertake to plant a colony there of fifty souls, upwards of fifteen years old; one-fourth part within one year, and within three years after the sending of the first, making together four years, the remainder, to the full number of fifty persons. . . .

The Company promises the colonists of the Patroons that they shall be free from customs, taxes, excise, imposts or any other contributions for the space of ten years; and after the expiration of the said ten years, at the highest, such customs as the goods pay here for the present. . . .

From all judgments given by the Courts of the Patroons for upwards of fifty guilders, there may be an appeal to the Company's Commander and Council in New Netherland. . . .

In regard to such private persons as on their own account, . . . shall be inclined to go there and settle, they shall, with the approbation of the Director and Council there, be at liberty to take up as much land as they shall be able properly to improve. . . .

Whosoever shall discover any shores, bays or other fit places for erecting fisheries, or the making of salt ponds may take possession thereof, and begin to work on them as their own absolute property. And it is consented to that the Patroons of colonists may send ships along the coast of New Netherland, on the cod fishery. . .

Whoever shall settle any colony out of the limits of the Manhattes Island, shall be obliged to satisfy the Indians for the land they shall settle upon, and they may extend or enlarge the limits of their colonies if they settle a proportionate number of colonists thereon.

The Patroons and colonists shall in the speediest manner, endeavor to find out ways and means whereby they may support a minister and schoolmaster that thus the service of God and zeal for religion may not grow cool and be neglected among them, and they shall, for the first, procure a comforter of the sick there. . . .

The colonists shall not be permitted to make any woolen, linen or cotton cloth, nor weave any other stuffs there, on pain of being banished, and as perjurers, to be arbitrarily punished. . . .

The Company will use their endeavors to supply the colonists with as many Blacks as they conveniently can, on the conditions hereafter to be made, in such manner, however, that they shall not be bound to do it for a longer time than they shall think proper. . . .

NEW AMSTERDAM - 1661

In September, 1661, an excellent description of the city was written under the title of "Description of Ye Towne of Mannadens in New Netherland." What follows is a portion of that account.

(Source: I.N. Phelps Stokes, ed., The Iconography of Manhattan Island, 1498-1909, I, New York, 1915-1926.) (The original is owned by the Royal Society of London.)

The Easter-side of the town is from the North-Eastgate onto the point whereon the Governor's new house stands. . . . Between the gate and the point the ground falls a little out and in, on this side of the town-gate, there is a (canal), whereby at high water boats go into the town, also on this side stand the Stathouse, before which is built a half moon of stone, where are mounted three small brass guns. . . .

The Souther-side or roundhead of the town is bounded with the arm of the sea. . . . Nearest the Wester-side of this head is a plot of ground a little higher than the other ground: on which stands a windmill: and a Fort four square, 100 yards on each side, at each corner flanked out 26 yards. . . . In this fort is the Church, the governors house, and houses for soldiers, ammunition, etc. . . . Within the town, in the midway between the N.W. corner and N.E. gate the ground has a small descent on each side much alike, and so continues through the town into the arm of the water on the Easter-side of the Town; by the help of this descent they have made a (canal) almost through the town, keyed it on both sides with timber and boards as far in as the three small bridges; and near the coming into the (canal) they have built two firm timber bridges with rails on each side; at low water the (canal) is dry; at high water boats come into it, passing under the two bridges, and go as far as the three small bridges. . . .

The town lies about forty degrees latitude, has good air, and is healthy, inhabited with several sorts of trades-men and merchants and mariners, where by it has much trade, of beaver--otter, musk--and other skins from the Indians and from the other towns in the River and Country inhabitants there-abouts. . . .

THE DUKE'S LAWS - 1665

Governor Richard Nicolls, the first English Governor of New York, issued a series of laws for the newly conquered colony. The English form of local government was substituted for the Dutch, while the limits of New York City were defined, among other provisions of the code.

(Source: The Colonial Laws of New York, I, New York, 1894.)

CAPITAL LAWS

1. If any person within this government shall by direct, expressed, impious or presumptuous ways deny the true God and His attributes, he shall be put to death.
2. If any person shall commit any willful and premeditated murder, he shall be put to death.
5. If any man or woman shall lie with any beast or brute creature by carnal copulation, they shall be put to death, and the beast shall be burned.
6. If any man lieth with mankind as he lieth with a woman, they shall be put to death, unless the one party were forced or be under fourteen years of age, in which case he shall be punished at the discretion of the Court of Assizes.
10. If any man shall treacherously conspire or publicly attempt to invade or surprise any town or towns, fort or forts within this government, he shall be put to death.

CHURCH

1. That in each parish within this government a church be built in the most convenient part thereof, capable to receive and accommodate two hundred persons.
2. That for the making and proportioning (of) the levies and assessments for building and repairing the churches, provision for the poor, maintenance for the minister, as well as for the more orderly managing of all parochial affairs in other cases expressed, eight of the most able men of each parish be by the major part of the householders of the said parish chosen to be overseers, out of which number the constable and the aforesaid eight overseers shall yearly make choice of two of the said number to be churchwardens. And in case of the death of any of the said overseers and churchwardens or his or their departure out of the parish, the said constable and overseers shall make choice of another to supply his room. . . .
4. To prevent scandalous and ignorant pretenders to the ministry from intruding themselves as teachers, no minister shall be admitted to officiate within the government but such as shall produce testimonials to the Governor that he hath received ordination either from some Protestant bishop or minister within some part of his Majesty's dominions, or the dominions of any foreign prince of the Reformed religion.

Upon which testimony the Governor shall induce the said minister into the parish that shall make presentation of him, as duly elected by the major part of the inhabitants householders.

6. No minister shall refuse the sacrament of baptism to the children of Christian parents when they shall be tendered, under penalty of loss of preferment.

9. Sundays are not to be profaned by travelers, laborers, or vicious persons.

11. No person of scandalous or vicious life shall be admitted to the holy sacrament who hath not given satisfaction therein to the minister.

CHILDREN AND SERVANTS

The constable and overseers are strictly required frequently to admonish the inhabitants of instructing their children and servants in matters of religion and the laws of the country and that parents and masters do bring up their children and apprentices in some honest lawful calling, labor, or employment. And if any children or servants become rude, stubborn, or unruly, refusing to hearken to the voice of their parents or masters, the constable and overseers (where no justice of peace shall happen to dwell within ten miles of the said town or parish) have power, upon the complaint of their parents or masters to call before them such an offender and to inflict such corporal punishment as the merit of their fact in their judgment shall deserve, not exceeding ten stripes, provided that such children and servants be of sixteen years of age.

OFFICERS AND OFFICES

All sheriffs, undersheriffs, or high constables and constables shall be changed every year. Only the undersheriffs or high constables, by special warrant, may continue in their office.

Justices of the peace are to continue in their places during ("their good behavior and" in some copies) the Governor's pleasure.

Clerks of courts, criers, and marshalls are to continue in their places during their good behavior, for breach of which they are punishable by the loss of their places and fine at the discretion of the court.

That the Governor and council may be special warrant displace any officer made or chosen within this government for neglecting of his office or other notorious misdemeanor and misbehavior. In which case the constable and overseers of any town shall proceed to a new election to supply the vacancy as if the said officer were dead, according to the rules prescribed for election of town officers.

OVERSEERS

Overseers shall be eight in number, men of good fame and life, chosen by the plurality of voices of the freeholders in each town, whereof four shall remain in their office two years successively, and four shall be changed for new ones every year; which election shall precede the elections of constables in point of time. In regard the constable for the year ensuing is to be chosen out of that number which are dismissed from their office of overseers. . . .

THE DONGAN CHARTER - 1686

The Dongan Charter, the second English Charter for New York City, was granted by Governor Thomas Dongan on April 27, 1686. It granted the Mayor, Aldermen, and commonalty additional privileges.

(Source: <u>The Colonial Laws of New York</u>, I, New York, 1894.)

...WHEREAS the Citty of New Yorke is an antient Citty within the said Province And the Cittizens of the said Citty have antiently been a Body Politique and Corporate and the Cittizens of the said Citty have held used and Enjoyed as well within the same as elsewhere in the said Province Diverse and Sundry Rights Libertyes Privilidges franchises ffree Customes Preheminences Advantages Jurisdiccons Emoluments and Immunityes as well by prescripcon as by Charter Letters Patents, Grants and Confirmacons not only of Divers Governours and Commanders in Cheife in the said Province butt alsoe of Severall Governours Directors Generalls and Commanders in Chiefe of the Neither Dutch Nation whilst the same was or has beene under their Power and Subjeccon AND WHEREAS Divers Lands Tennements and Heriditaments Jurisdiccons Libertyes Immunityes and Privilidges have heretofore been Given... to the Cittizens and Inhabitants of the said City sometimes by the name of Scout Burgomasters and Schepens of the City of New Amsterdam and sometimes by the name of the Mayor Aldermen and Commonality of the City of New Yorke...AND WHEREAS the Cittizens and Inhabitants of the said Citty have erected...at their owne Proper Costs and Charges several Publique Buildings Accommodations and Conveniences for the said Citty... the Citty Hall or State House with the Ground thereunto belonging two Markett Houses the Bridge into the Dock the Wharfes or Dock with their appurtenances and the New Buriall place without the Gate of the Citty and have Established and Settled one ffery from the said Citty of New Yorke to Long Island...KNOW YEE that I the said Thomas Dongan by Virtue of the Comicon and Authority unto me Given...at the humble Peticon of the now Mayor Aldermen and Commonalty of the Said Citty of New Yorke...for and on the behalfe of his most Sacred Majesty... Doe Give...unto the said Mayor Aldermen and Commonaly of the said Citty all and every such and the same Libertyes Privilidges and franchises Rights Royaltyes, ffree Customes Jurisdiccons and Immunityes which they...have antiently had...PROVIDED Alwayes that none of the (same)...be inconsistant with...the Laws of his Majestyes Kingdome of England or any other the Laws of the Generall Assembly of this Province and the aforesaid Publique Buildings Addommodacons and Conveniencyes...together with all the Proffitts...which...may Accrue ...hereafter for Dockage or Warfage within the said Dock with all and Singular the Rents...which shall...Arise Grow or Accrue... and also all...the Streets Lanes Highwayes & Alleys within the said

Citty of New Yorke and Manhatans Island...togather with full Power ...to...Direct the Establishing...& Repairing of all Streets Lanes Allyes Highwayes Water Courses fferry and Bridges in and through out the said Citty of New Yorke and Manhatans Island aforesaid... PROVIDED alwayes that this said Lycence...be not Extended... to the takeing Away of any Person or Persons Right or Property without his her or their consent or by some knowne Law of the said Province ...AND I Doe by these p'sents...Confirme unto the said Mayor Aldermen and Commonalty of the said Citty of New Yorke and their Successors forever the Royaltyes of Fishing Fowleing, Hunting, Hawkeing Mineralls...(Gold and Silver Mines only excepted) TO have...for ever RENDRING...unto his...Majesty...Yearly forever hereafter the Annuall Quitt Rent...of one Bever Skin or the Value thereof in Currant Mony of this Province...AND...I...Declare that the said Citty of New Yorke...and the Jurisdiccon of the same shall from henceforth extend (limits given) AND also I doe for and on the behalfe of his most Sacred Majesty...Grant...that for the better Governmt of the said Citty...their shall be forever hereafter within the said Citty a Mayor and Recorder Towne Clerke and six Assistants...who shall be forever hereafter Called the Mayor Alermen and Commonaltye of the City of New Yorke and that there shall be forever one Chamberlaine or Treasurer one Sherriffe one Coroner one Clerke of the Markett one High Constable seven Sub constables and one Marshall or Serjant at Mace...AND I Doe...Declare...the Mayor Recorder and Aldermen and Assistants of the said Citty of New Yorke for the time being and their Successors forever hereafter (to be)...one Body Corporate and Politique ...(which) may for ever hereafter have one Common Seale. (He then authorizes the existing officers to act until successors are chosen: Nicholas Bayard, mayor; James Graham, recorder; John West, town clerk; Andrew Bowne, John Robinson, William Beakeman, John Delavall, Abraham Depeister, and Johannes Kipp, aldermen; and Nicholas Demeter, Johannes VanBrugh, John De Bruyne, Teunisse Decay, Abraham Corbett, and Wolfert Webber, assistants AND I Doe by these presents Grant... that the Mayor Recorder Aldermen and Assistants of the said Citty... or the Mayor Recorder and any three or more of the Aldermen and any three or more of the Assistants...shall be called the Comon Councell of the said Citty And that they or the Greater Parte of them shall... have full Power...to Call...Comon Councell...and their as occasion shall be to make Laws Order Ordinances and Constitutions in Writeing and to add Alter Diminish or Reforme them from time to time as to them shall seem Necessary...and which Laws...shall be...in force for the space of Three Months and noe longer Unlesse they shall be Allowed of and Confirmed by the Governor and Councell...the Appointment of the Mayor and Sherriffe...shall bee as followeth...upon the feast day of St. Michael the Archangell Yearly the Leiuetenant Governour or Commander in Ehiefe for the time being by and with the Advice of his Councell shall Nominate and Appointe such Person as he shall thinke fitte to be Mayor...for the Yeare next ensueing and one other Person...to be Sherriffe...AND further that According to the new Usage and Custome of the said Citty the Recorder Towne Clerk & Clerk of ye Markett...

shall be...such Person as the Lieut. Governour...shall appointe... According to the Tenour and effect of their said Commissions... AND further...the Mayor and Recorder...and three or more of the Aldermen of the said Citty not exceeding five shall be Justice and keepers of the Peace...(to hear petty cases: petty larceny, riots, routs, oppressions, extortions, trespasses) AND moreover I Doe...Appoint that the Aldermen Assistants High Constable and Petty Constables within the Citty be Yearly Chosen on the feast Day of St. Michael...for ever...one Alderman one assistant and one Constable for each Respective ward and one Constable for each Division in the out Ward in such Publique Place in the said Respective Wards as the Aldermen for...each Ward shall Direct and Appoint and that the Aldermen Assistants and Petty Constables be Chosen by Majority of Voices of the Inhabitants of each ward and that the High Constable be Appointed by the Mayor of the said Citty for the time being AND that the Chamberlaine shall be Yearly Chosen on the said ffeast Day...by the Mayor Aldermen and Assistants (On behalf of the king, empowers sheriff, constables, and others to send offenders to jail) AND...grant...that the said Mayor of the said Citty and noe other (according to usage...) shall have Power and Authority to...Grant Lycences Annually...to all Tavern keepers (etc.)... not exceeding the Sume of thirty Shillings for each Lycence All which Mony...shall be used and Applyed to the Publique use of the said Mayor Aldermen and Commonalty of the said City of New Yorke and their Successors without any Account thereof to be Rendered...to any of the Lieutenants or Governours of this Province...AND know yee that ...the Mayor Recorder and Aldermen or the Mayor and any three or more of the Aldermen...shall...have full Power and Authority... to make ffree Cittizens of the said Citty and Libertyes thereof and noe Person or Persons whatsoever other then such ffree Cittizens shall hereafter use any art trade Mistory or Manuall Occupacon within the said Citty Libertyes and Precincts thereof Sayeing in the time of faires ...only (on pain of having shop closed, fines imposed, without account of same to governors) PROVIDED that noe Person...shall be made free (without meeting certain qualifications of naturalization)...and Doe pay for the Publique use of the said Mayor Aldermen and Comonalty... such...Mony as heretofore hath been...Accustomed to paid...on their being Admitted ffreemen...Provided it is not exceeding the sume of five Pounds (Mayor, aldermen, and commonalty may purchase lands not to exceed the value of one thousand pounds yearly and to dispose of same at will. They and their successors) shall...hold...within the said Citty in every weeke of the yeare three Markett Days the one upon Tuesday the other upon Thursday and the other on Saturday Weekly...may att any time...fill...the Land...in and about the said Citty...and Build upon or make use of in any other manner...as to them shall seem fitt ...AND I doe...Grant unto the aforesaid & Mayor Aldermen and Comonalty...that they and their Successors shall...keep within the said Citty and Libertyes and Precincts thereof in every weeke in every Yeare for ever upon Tuesday one Court of Common Pleas...the same to be held before the Mayor Recorder and Aldermen or any three of them whereof the Mayor or Recorder to be one (additional grant of all powers enjoyed by mayor, aldermen, and commonalty for past twenty years provided they be not repugnant to laws of England or of the General Assembly of the province).

THE MONTGOMERIE CHARTER - 1731

On February 11, 1731, Governor John Montgomerie granted New York City a new charter. It expanded the powers of the local government. A portion of the charter follows.

(Source: E.B. O'Callaghan, <u>Documents Relative to the Colonial History of the State of New York</u>, II, Albany, 1856.)

. . . .In order thereunto, we have thought fit, them, the said inhabitants and citizens of the said city of New York, (by whatsoever name or names they have been or were incorporated, or whether they have been or were heretofore incorporated or not) into one body politic and corporate, by the name of the mayor, aldermen and commonalty of the city of New York, by out letters to make, constitute, confim, renew and of new to create. And we, being also further willing fully intending and desiring that the said inhabitants and citizens of our said city, by the name aforesaid, should have perpetual succession, and should hold, possess and enjoy, all and singular, the rights, privileges, liberties, franchises, pre-eminences, advantages, jurisdictions, courts, powers, offices, authorities, ferries, fees, fines, prequisites, profits, immunities, rents, possessions, lands, tenements and other hereditaments, not only which in the before recited grants, confirmations, writings and letters patent are mentioned, or intended to be thereby granted, but also, which they have held or claim to hold, by prescription or otherwise, with the alterations and enlargements thereof and additions thereto, in such manner and form as hereafter is mentioned and contained, notwithstanding the before mentioned or any other question, doubts, opinions, ambiguities, debates, faults, or imperfections.

1. Wherefore know ye, That we of our especial grace, certain knowledge and meer motion, have willed, ordained, constituted, confirmed, given, and granted, and by these presents for us, our heirs and successors do will, ordain, constitute, confirm, give and grant, that our said city of New York be, and from henceforth forever hereafter shall be and remain a free city of itself; and that the mayor, aldermen and commonalty of the said city, and their successors from henceforth forever alty of the said city, and their successors from henceforth forever hereafter shall be and remain one body corporate and politic, in re-facto and nomine, by the name of the mayor, aldermen and commonalty of the city of New York, and them and their successors by the name of the mayor, aldermen and commonalty of the city of New York, one body corporate, in re-facto and nomine, really and fully, we do for us, our heirs and successors, erect, make, ordain, constitute, confirm, declare and create, by these presents, and that by that name they shall and may have perpetual succession; and also, that they and their successors, by the said name of the mayor, aldermen and commonalty of the city of New York be, and forever hereafter shall be persons able in law, and capable to sue and be sued, implead and be impleaded, answer and be answered unto, defend and be defended, in all courts and places before us, our heirs and succes-

sors, and elsewhere in all and all manner of actions, suits, complaints, pleas, causes, matters, and demands whatsoever, and of what kind or nature soever, in as full and ample manner and form as any of our other liege subjects of our said province, being persons able and capable in law, can or may sue and be sued, implead and be impleaded, answer and be answered unto, defend and be defended, by any lawful ways and means whatsoever. And also, That they and their successors, by the name of the mayor, aldermen and commonalty of the city of New York, be and shall be forever hereafter, persons capable and able in law to purchase, take, hold, receive, enjoy and have any messuages, houses, buildings lands, tenements, rents, possessions and other hereditaments and real estate, within or without our said province, in fee and forever, or for time of life or lives or years, or in any other manner; and also goods, chattels and all other things of what kind or quality soever. And also, That they and their successors by the same name of the mayor, aldermen and commonalty of the city of New York, shall and may give, grant, demise, assign and sell, or otherwise dispose of all or any the messuages, houses, buildings lands, tenements, rents, possessions and other hereditaments and real estate, and all their goods, chattels and other things aforesaid as to them shall seem meet, at their own will and pleasure.

And also, That the said mayor, aldermen and commonalty of the city of New York, for the time being, and their successors shall and may forever hereafter, have and use a common seal for sealing all and singular deeds, grants, conveyances, contracts, bonds, articles of agreements, assignments, powers, authorities, and all and singular their affairs and things touching or concerning the said corporation. And, by virtue of these our letters, it shall and may be lawful to and for the said mayor, aldermen and commonalty of the city of New York and their successors, as they shall see cause, to break, change and new make the same, or any other common seal, when, and as often as to them it shall seem convenient.

2. And we do further, of our especial grace, certain knowledge and meer motion, for us, our heirs and successors, give grant, order and appoint that the said city of New York, and the compass, precincts, circuit, bounds, liberties and jurisdictions of the same do reach, extend and stretch forth, and shall and may reach, extend and stretch forth, as well in length as in breadth and circuit, in and through the limits and boundaries following, to wit: To begin at the river, creek or run of water called Spyt den Duyvel, over which King's bridge is built, where the said river or creek empties itself into the North river, on Westchester side thereof, at low-water-mark, and so to run along the said river, creek or run, on Westchester side, at low-water-mark, unto the East river or Sound, and from thence to cross over to Nassau Island, to low-water-mark there, including Great Barn Island, Little Barn Island and Manning's Island, and from thence all along Nassau Island shore, at low-water-mark, unto the south side of Red Hook; and from thence to run a line across the North river, so as to include Nutton Island, Bedlow's Island, Bucking Island and the Oyster Island, . . .

GASLIGHT COMES TO NEW YORK - 1826

In 1823, the New York Gas Light Company was chartered. By 1824, the first house in New York was lighted by gas. In 1826, the Common Council appointed a committee to investigate the possibility of introducing gas light into the streets. The excerpt that follows is part of the report filed by the committee.

(Source: New York City Common Council, <u>Report of a Special Committee on Gas Light</u>, New York, 1826.)

IN COMMON COUNCIL,

JUNE 29, 1826.

The following Report of the Special Committee on Gas Light, was presented, and directed to be printed for the use of the members.

J. MORTON, Clerk.

The Special Committee, to whom was referred a resolution of the 13th February last, directing enquiries into the expense of introducing the Gas Light into the streets of this city,

REPORT,

That they have been furnished with a copy of the contract between the New-York Gas Light Company and the Corporation of this city; by this contract, the company engage to furnish all pipes, and necessary conductors to the foot of the lamp post, and the city is to supply or pay for, the lamp posts, lamps, lamp irons, conductors through the post, and other "fitting up," and to put down the posts at their expense, and are to be "at no other expense for fixtures, conductors, repairs, or on any other account whatsoever." There is however, a clause in the agreement, on which the company claim to be bound only to keep in repair the "pipes and conductors;" on this point your committee have come to no decision with them, but they do not deem it important that this should be insisted on as preliminary, as it will have no material operation on the proposition they will submit.

The company are to light "all and every of the public streets or parts of streets, lying and being south of a line commencing at the East River, at the foot of Grand-street, and running through Grand-street to Sullivan-street, and through Sullivan-street, to Canal-street, and through Canal-street to the North River," and they engage to be ready to light the street

Broadway, on the 12th day of May 1825, and all the other parts of the city, included in their contract on the 12th day of May 1828; it appears by a communication in possession of your committee, that the Corporation were informed by the company prior to the time specified in the contract, that they were ready to light Broadway.

Information gathered from experience in England and this country, convinces your committee that posts of wood are not suitable, the aperture required at the bottom being so large as to weaken the post very much, subjects it to rot, and renders it difficult to keep it erect and firm in the ground, they therefore recommend the use of iron posts, believing that in addition to their superiority, they should be used on the score of economy; in narrow streets however, they would advise the use of iron brackets secured against the sides of buildings, and extending out at least five feet.

Your committee have seen a pattern post, less in size and weight, than those already erected in the streets by the Gas Company, which they believe to be sufficiently large, and have ascertained the lowest price that they can be obtained for.

The following is the estimated cost of one lamp and fixtures.

Iron post to weigh 3cwt at $70 per ton,	$10 50
Lead tubing, through the post (10 feet0	1 84
Jet, cock and pillar, - - -	0 93
Lanthorn and lamp iron, - - -	4 50
Putting down post, - - -	0 50
Total,	$18 27

There may be a small addition to the cost of the lanthorn, as named above, but your committee believe, they will be safe in estimating the w whole cost to be Twenty Dollars per lamp.

There are in the city at present, 2,748 lamps. In the diestrict included in the contract with the Gas Company there are but 1,849, these are in general much too far apart, and the city cannot be lighted properly (even with gas) in the opinion of your committee, without increasing the number to 2,400, the distances varying in the populous part of the city from 100 to 160 feet, while it is found that in London and Liverpool, they are placed f from 60 to 90 feet apart, according to the width of the street; it is believed however, that in our atmosphere, the streets will be sufficiently light, if the posts are placed 100 feet apart in those streets not wider than Broadway.

On the supposition, that it will require 2,400 lamps in the district contracted for with the Gas Company, and assuming the cost of one lamp to be correct, as estimated by your committee, the total expenditure required would be $48,000; it must however be taken into consideration, that the 1,849 Oil Lamps to be taken up, are, or will be all wanted for the upper wards of the city; their ascertained cost when new is $9 62 -- allowing them to be worth $7, they would amount to $12,943, leaving the whole actual expenditure at $37,057, from which may be deducted the saving to be made by using brackets in narrow streets.

But your Committee deem it important to call your attention to the fact, that it will probably be at least three years before the whole expenditure will be required, and that it is optional with the Corporation how far the city shall be lighted.

With a view to test the value of gas light, before the whole contract is entered into, they recommend that Broadway be lit with the same from Grand-street to the Battery, the present season; considering that it will be a peculiarly fit time to set about it, as it is contemplated to re-pave that street . . .

Resolved, That it is expedient to enter upon the contract with the New-York Gas Light Company, so far as to have Broadway from Grand-street to the Battery lit by them, without unnecessary delay.

A CHARTER AMENDMENT ACT - 1830

As New York's population and area increased during the first half of the nineteenth century, the State Legislature recognized the necessity of providing the city with a more autonomous government. As a result, in 1830, a major change in the operations of the government of the City of New York took place. What follows is a portion of the Act to Amend the Charter of New York, that incorporated these changes.

(Source: New York State Legislature, <u>Documents</u>, "An Act to Amend the Charter of the City of New York," April 17, 1830.

1. The legislative power of the Corporation of the City of New York, shall be vested in a board of Aldermen and a board of Assistants, who together shall form the Common Council of the City.

2. Each Ward of the City shall be entitled to elect one person to be denominated the Alderman of the Ward, and the persons so chosen, together shall form the board of Aldermen; and each Ward shall also be entitled to elect one person to be denominated an Assistant Alderman; and the persons so chosen, together shall form the board of Assistants.

3. The Aldermen and Assistant Aldermen shall be chosen for one year; and no person shall be eligible to either office, who shall not, at the time of his election, be a resident of the ward for which he is chosen.

4. The annual election for Charter Officers shall commence on the second Tuesday in April, and the Officers elected shall be sworn into office on the second Tuesday in May thereafter; and all the provisions of law now in force in regard to the notification, duration, and conduct of elections for Members of Assembly, and in regard to the appointment, powers and duties of the inspectors holding the same, shall apply to the annual election of Charter Officers.

5. The first election for Charter Officers, after the passage of this law, shall take place on the second Tuesday in April, one thousand eight hundred and thirty-one; and all those persons who shall have been elected under the former laws regulating the election of Charter Officers, and shall be in office at the time of the passage of this law, shall continue in office until the officers elected under this law shall be entitled to be sworn into office.

6. The board of Aldermen shall have power to direct a special election to be held, to supply the place of any Alderman whose seat shall become vacant by death, removal from the city, resignation, or otherwise; and the board of Assistants shall also have power to direct a special elec-

tion to supply any vacancy that may occur in the board of Assistants; and in both cases, the person elected to supply the vacancy, shall hold his seat only for the residue of the term of office of his immediate predecessor.

7. The boards shall meet in separate chambers, and a majority of each shall be a quorum to do business. Each board shall appoint a President from its own body, and shall also choose its Clerk and other officers, determine the rules of its own proceedings, and be the judge of the qualifications of its own members. Each board shall keep a journal of its proceedings, and the doors of each shall be kept open, except when the public welfare shall require secrecy; and all resolutions and reports of Committees which shall recommend any specific improvement involving the appropriation of public monies, or taxing or assessing the citizens of said city, shall be published immediately after the adjournment of the board, under the authority of the Common Council, in all the newspapers employed by the Corporation: and whenever a vote is taken in relation thereto, the ayes and noes shall be called and published in the same manner.

8. Each board shall have the authority to compel the attendance of absent members; to punish its members for disorderly behaviour, and to expel a member, with the concurrence of two-thirds of the members elected to the board; and the member so expelled, shall, by such expulsion, forfeit all his right and powers as an Alderman or Assistant Alderman.

9. The stated and occasional meetings of each board of Common Council, shall be regulated by its own ordinances; and both boards may meet on the same or on different days as they may severally judge expedient.

10. Any law, ordinance, or resolution of the Common Council may originate in either board, and when it shall have passed one board, may be rejected or amended by the other.

11. No member of either board shall, during the period for which he was elected, be appointed to, or be competent to hold any office, of which the emoluments are paid from the city treasury, or by fees, directed to be paid by any ordinance or act of the Common Council, or be directly or indirectly interested in any contract, the expenses or consideration whereof are to be paid under any ordinance of the Common Council; but this section shall not be construed to deprive any Alderman or Assistant of any emoluments or fees which he is entitled to, by virtue of his office.

12. Every act, ordinance, or resolution, which shall have passed the two boards of the Common Council, before it shall take effect, shall be presented, duly certified, to the Mayor of the City, for his approbation. If he approve, he shall sign it; if not, he shall return it with his objections to the board in which it originated, within ten days thereafter; or if such board be not then in session, at its next stated meeting. The board to which it shall be returned, shall enter the objections at large on their journal, and cause the same to be published in one or more of the public newspapers of the city.

13. The board to which such act, ordinance, or resolution, shall

after the expiration of not less than ten days thereafter, proceed to re-consider the same. If after such re-consideration, a majority of the members elected to the board shall agree to pass the same, it shall be sent, together with the objections, to the other board, by which it shall be likewise re-considered; and if approved by a majority of all the members elected to such board, it shall take effect as an act or law of the Corporation. In all such cases the votes of both boards shall be determined by yeas and nays, and the names of the persons voting for and against the passage of the measure reconsidered, shall be entered on the journal of each board respectively.

14. If the Mayor shall not return any act, ordinance, or resolution, so presented to him, within the time above limited for that purpose, it shall take effect in the same manner as if he had signed it.

15. Neither the Mayor nor Recorder of the City of New-York, shall be a member of the Common Council thereof, after the second Tuesday of May, one thousand eight hundred and thirty-one.

16. Whenever there shall be a vacancy in the office of Mayor, and whenever the Mayor shall be absent from the city, or be prevented by sickness, or any other cause, from attending to the duties of his office, the President of the board of Aldermen shall act as Mayor, and shall possess all the rights and powers of the Mayor, during the continuance of such vacancy, absence, or disability . . . .

17. It shall be the duty of the Mayor,

First. -- To communicate to the Common Council, at least once a year, and oftener if he shall deem it expedient, a general statement of the situation and condition of the City, in relation to its government, finances and improvements.

Second. -- To recommend to the adoption of the Common Council all such measures connected with the police, security, health, cleanliness, and ornament of the City, and the improvement of its government, and finances, as he shall deem expedient.

Third. -- To be vigilant and active in causing the laws and ordinances of the government of the City to be duly executed and enforced.

Fourth. -- To exercise a constant supervision and controul over the conduct and acts of all subordinate officers, and to receive and examine into all such complaints as may be prefered against any of them for violation or neglect of duty, and generally to perform all such duties as may be prescribed to him by the Charter and city ordinances, and the Laws of this State and the United States.

18. Annual and occasional appropriations shall be made by proper ordinances of the Common Council, for every branch and object of city expenditure, nor shall any money be drawn from the city treasury except the same shall have been previously appropriated to the purpose for which it is drawn.

19. The Common Council shall not have authority to borrow any sums of money whatever on the credit of the Corporation, except in anticipation of the revenue of the year in which such loan shall be made; unless authorized by a special act of the legislature. . . .

CREATION OF THE PUBLIC SCHOOLS - 1842

The State Legislature, on April 11, 1842, passed an act creating the first organized and regulated public school system for the city. A New York City Board of Education was also established for the first time. This act follows.

(Source: Laws of New York, Albany, 1842.)

The People of the State of New York, represented in Senate and Assembly, do enact as follows:

§ 1. There shall be elected in each of the wards of the city and county of New York two commissioners, two inspectors and five trustees of common schools, who shall be elected by ballot, at a special election to be held on the first Monday of June in each year, by the persons qualified to vote for charter officers in the said wards, and to be conducted in the same manner, by the same inspectors, at the same ward districts, and subject to the same laws, rules and regulations, as now govern the charter elections in said city. The commissioners of common schools so elected shall constitute a board of education for the city of New-York; a majority of whom shall constitute a quorum. They shall elect one of their number president of said board, who shall preside at the meetings thereof, which shall be held at least as often as once in three months, and they may appoint a clerk, whose compensation shall be fixed and paid by the supervisors of said city and county. The commissioners so elected in each ward shall be the commissioners of schools thereof, with the like powers and duties of commissioners of common schools in the several towns in this state, except as hereinafter provided. The said inspectors of common schools so elected in the several wards shall have the like powers, and be subject to the same duties with the inspectors of common schools of the several towns of this state, except as hereinafter provided. The trustees of common schools so elected in their respective wards shall be the trustees of the school districts, which may be formed and organized therein, with the like powers and durites as the trustees of school districts in the several towns in this state, except as hereinafter provided.

§ 2. All such provisions of the third, fourth, fifth, and sixth articles of Title two, Chapter fifteen, Part first of the Revised Statutes, and of the several acts amending, and in addition to and relating to the same, not inconsistent with the provisions in this act contained, shall be, and the same are, hereby declared applicable to the city and county of New-York.

§ 3. For all the purposes of this act, each of the several wards into which the said city and county of New-York now is or may be hereafter divided, shall be considered as a separate town, and liable to all the duties imposed, and entitled to all the powers, privileges, immunities, and advantages granted by the said third, fourth, fifth, and sixth Articles of Title two, Chapter fifteen, Part first of the Revised Statutes, to the several towns in this state, so far as the same are consistent with this act.

§ 4. The forty-fourth section of the act entitled "An act to amend the second Title of the fifteenth Chapter of the first Part of the Revised Statutes, relating to common schools," passed May 26, 1841, is hereby repealed; and all the other sections of the said act, not inconsistent with the provisions of this act, are hereby declared applicable to the city and county of New-York.

§ 5. No compensation shall be allowed to the commissioners, inspectors, or trustees of common schools for any services performed by them, but the commissioners and inspectors shall receive their actual and reasonable expenses while attending to the duties of their office, to be audited and allowed by the supervisors of said city and county.

§ 6. The said commissioners of common schools of each ward are hereby authorized to appoint a clerk, whose compensation shall be settled and paid by the board of supervisors.

§ 7. Whenever the trustees elected in any ward shall certify in writing to the commissioners and inspectors of common schools thereof, that it is necessary to organize one or more schools in said ward, in addition to the schools mentioned in the thirteenth section of this act, it shall be the duty of said commissioners and inspectors to meet together and examine into the facts and circumstances of the case; and if they shall be satisfied of such necessity, they shall certify the same under their hands to the said board of education, and shall then proceed to organize one or more school districts therein, and shall procure a school house and all things necessary to organize a school in such district, the expense of which shall be levied and raised pursuant to the provisions of section nine of this act; and the ti title to all lands purchased by virtue of this act, with the buildings thereon, shall be vested in the city and county of New-York.

§ 8. Whenever the clerk of the city and county of New-York shall receive notice from the superintendent of common schools, of the amount of moneys apportioned to the city and county of New-York, for the support and encouragement of common schools therein, he shall immediately lay the same before the supervisors of the city and county aforesaid.

§ 9. The said supervisors shall annually raise and collect, by tax upon the inhabitants of said city and county, a sum of money equal to the sum specified in such notice, at the same time and in the same manner as the contingent charges of the said city and county are levied and collected; also a sum of money equal to one-twentieth of one per cent of the value of real and personal property in the said city liable to be assessed therein, to be applied exclusively to the purposes of common schools in said city; and such further sum as may be necessary for the support and benefit of common schools in said city and county, to be raised, levied, and collected in like manner, and which shall be in lieu of all taxes and assessments to the support of common schools for said city and county.

§ 10. The said supervisors shall, on or before the first day of May in every year, direct that a sum of money equal to the amount last received by the chamberlain of said city and county from the common school fund, be deposited by him, together with the sum so received from the school fund, in one of the incorporated banks in the said city and county, (such bank to be designated by the said supervisors,) to the credit of the commissioners of common schools in each of the said several wards, in the proportions to which they shall respectively be entitled, and subject only to the drafts of the said commissioners respectively, who shall pay the amount apportioned to the several schools enumerated in the thirteenth section of this act, to the treasurer of the societies or schools entitled thereto, or to some person duly authorized by the trustees of such societies or schools to receive the same.

§ 11. So much of the seventh Article of Title second, Chapter fifteen, Part first of the Revised Statutes, and the several acts amending and in addition to, and relating to the said article as is specially applicable to the city and county of New-York, and all other acts, and all provisions therein, providing for or directing, or concerning the disbursing or appropriation of the funds created for or applicable to common school education in the city and county of New-York, and all and every provision for raising any fund, or for the imposition of any tax therefor, so far as the same are inconsistent with this act, are hereby repealed.

§ 12. All children between the ages of four and sixteen, residing in said city and county, shall be entitled to attend any of the common schools therein; and the parents, guardians, or other persons having the custody or care of such children, shall not be liable to any tax, assessment, or imposition for the tuition of any such children, other than is herein before provided.

§ 13. The schools of the Public School Society, the New-York Orphan Asylum school, the Roman Catholic Orphan Asylum school, the schools of the two Half Orphan Asylums, the school of the Mechanics' School Society, the Harlem school, the Yorkville Public school, the Manhattanville Free school, the Hamilton Free school, the Institution for the Blind, the school connected with the alms house of the said city, and the school of the Association for the Benefit of Colored Orphans, shall be subject to the general jurisdiction of the said commissioners of the respective wards in which any of the said schools now are or hereafter may be located, subject to the direction of the board of education, but under the immediate govemment and management of their respective trustees, managers, and directors, in the same manner and to the same extent as herein provided in respect to the district schools, herein first before mentioned, in said city and county; and so far as relates to the distribution of the common school moneys, each of the said schools shall be district schools of the said city.1

§ 14. No school above mentioned, or which shall be organized under this act, in which any religious sectarian doctrine or tenet shall be taught, inculcated, or practised, shall receive any portion of the school moneys to be distributed by this act, as hereinafter provided; and it shall be the duty of the trustees, inspectors, and commissioners of schools in eash ward, and of the deputy superintendent of schools, from time to time, and as frequently as need be, to examine and ascertain, and report to the said board of education, whether any religious sectarian doctrine or tenet shall have been taught, inculcated, or practised in any of the schools in their respective wards; and it shall be the duty of the commissioners of schools in the several wards to transmit to the board of education, all reports made to them by the trustees and inspectors of their respective wards. The board of education and any number thereof, may at any time visit and examine any school subject to the provisions of this act, and individual commissioners shall report to the board the result of their examinations.

§ 15. It shall be the duty of the said board of education to apply, for the use of the several districts, such moneys as shall be raised to erect, purchase, or lease school houses, or to procure the sites therefor; and also, to apportion among the several schools and districts provided for by th this act, the school moneys to be paid over to the commissioners of schools in each ward, by virtue of the tenth section of this act, and shall file with the chamberlain of said city and county, on or before the fifteenth day of Apri April, in each year, a copy of such apportionment, and stating the amount thereof to be paid to the commissioners of each ward; which apportionment shall be made among the said several schools and districts, according to the average number of children over four and under sixteen years of age, who shall have actually attended such school the preceding year. But no such school shall be entitled to a portion of such moneys, that has not been kept open at least nine months in the year, or in which any religious sectarian doctrine or tenet shall have been taught, inculcated, or practised, or which shall refuse to permit the visits and examinations provided for by this act.

§ 16. The commissioners of schools of the respective wards, when they have received from the chamberlain of said city and county, the money apportioned to the several schools and districts in their several wards, sha shall apply the same to the use of the schools and districts in their several wards, according to the apportionment thereof so made by the said board of education.

§ 17. The said commissioners of each ward shall, within fifteen days after their election, execute and deliver to the supervisors aforesaid, a bond with which such sureties as said supervisors shall approve, in the penalty of double the amount of public money appropriated to the use of the common schools of their respective wards, conditioned for the faithful performance of the duties of their office, and the proper application of all moneys coming in their hands for common school purposes. Such bond shall be filed by the said supervisors, in the office of the county clerk.

§ 18. This act shall take effect immediately.

THE CREATION OF THE POLICE DEPARTMENT - 1844

In 1844, the City abolished the old Watch Department, and organized in its place a day and night police force to number not more than eight hundred. An excerpt from this act, which went into effect in 1845, follows.

(Source: Board of Aldermen, Proceedings, vol. 26, May 13, 1844, New York, 1844.)

Appointments and Removals.

§ 1. "The Special Justices for Preserving the Peace, Clerks of Police, and Scriveners shall continue to be appointed in the manner now provided for by law, for the term, and removable in the manner therein prescribed.

§ 2. "The Captains and Assistant Captains of Patrol shall be appointed by the Common Council; they shall be citizens of the United States, of good and respectable character, of sound mind and body, of not less than twenty-one years, nor more than sixty years of age, and competent to the discharge of the duties of the office to which they shall severally be appointed; they may hold their respective offices during good behaviour, and shall be removable for corrupt, immoral, and licentious conduct, neglect of duty, incapacity, or any malpractice in office, by the Common Council, on complaint in writing, with the charges preferred, duly authenticated, which complaint shall be filed with the Mayor, and upon which the Mayor may immediately suspend the officer, so complained of, until the Board shall have acted on the complaint, the Mayor to investigate the charges,(giving the party complained of the opportunity of making his defence,) and communicating to the Common Council the opinion which he forms, as to the charges being sustained.

§ 3. "The Patrolmen shall be appointed by the Mayor, on the nomination of the several Captains of Patrol; they shall be possessed of the character and qualifications above prescribed, the Captains and Assistants may hold their appointments during good behaviour, and shall be removable for the like cause as the Captains and Assistants, as herein before provided for, by the Mayor, on complaint, as aforesaid, after due examination, and hearing the defence of the person complained of; and the several Captains shall have the power of suspending any person of their several patrols, for any of the above named causes, and for disobedience of orders; and each of the Captains, upon thus suspending any of his Patrol, shall immediately make his charges against the person to the Mayor, in writing, authenticated by his affidavit.

§ 4. "That Captains of Patrol shall keep each a book, in which shall be recorded the names of persons to act as Chancemen, or Substitutes for Patrolmen absent at roll call. No person to be put on such Chance list, unless possessing the character or qualifications required for Patrolmen, and approved by the Mayor; and when so placed on the list, to be taken in rotation, when required for duty, or when appointed to fill vacancy.

§ 5. "The Special Justices shall semi-annually (or oftener, if required,) report to the Common Council the state of the Police, its practical operation. together with such suggestions as seem to them proper to promote its efficiency, and the peace and good order of the City. The Captains of Patrol shall also report quarter yearly, (or whenever required,) to the Mayor, the state of their several patrols, and situation of their several districts, with regard to the preservation of good order therein, together with any suggestions that may appear to them necessary, to render their duties more efficient for the preservation of the peace of the City, and the protection of the persons and property of its citizens. . . ."

§ 1. "There shall be a Board of Appointment, to consist of the following persons: The Mayor, three Aldermen, and three Assistant Aldermen. The Aldermen and Assistant Aldermen, shall first be choson by ballot in their respective Boards, immediately after the passage of this Ordinance, and annually thereafter, at the first meeting in June. . . ."

"That a due proportion of the said Patrolment and Policemen, connected with the Police, shall be appointed from each Ward of said City, such proportion being ascertained by reference to the population of the Wards, respectively, which proportion for each Ward shall be appointed by the Mayor, on nomination of the Aldermen and Assistants of the Wards, respectively, from which they are selected.

THE GRISCOM REPORT - 1845

Health and sanitation problems have always
been of importance in New York City, although
the municipal administrations have not always
met their responsibilities concerning these
problems adequately, due to a lack of funds,
and a lack of knowledge. The following selection is a portion of a report dealing with these
problems, written by the city Inspector, Dr.
John H. Griscom.

(Source: John H. Griscom, The Sanitary Condition of the Laboring Population of New York, New York, 1845.)

. . .At all seasons of the year, there is an amount of sickness and death in this, as in all large cities, far beyond those of less densely peopled, more airy and open places, such as country residences. Even in villages of small size, there is an observable difference over the isolated country dwelling, in the proportionate amount of disease prevailing; proving conclusively that the congregation of animal and vegetable matters, with their constant effluvia, which has less chance of escape from the premises, is detrimental to the health of the inhabitants.

The circumstances have never yet been investigated in this city, as they should be. Our people, especially the more destitute, have been allowed to live out their brief lives in tainted and unwholesome atmospheres, and be subject to the silent and invisible encroachments of destructive agencies from every direction, without one warning voice being raised to point to them their danger, and without an effort to rescue them from their impending fate. Fathers are taken from their children, husbands from their wives, "ere they have lived out half their days," -- the widows and orphans are thrown upon public or private charity for support, and the money which is expended to save them from starvation, to educate them in the public schools, or, perchance, to maintain them in the work-house or the prison, if judiciously spent in improving the sanitary arrangements of the city, and instilling into the population a knowledge of the means by which their health would be protected, and their lives prolonged and made happy, would have been not only saved, but returned to the treasury in the increased health of the population, a much better state of public morals, and, by consequence, a more easily governed and respectable community.

It is of course among the poorer laboring classes that such knowledge is most wanted. The rich, though they may be equally ignorant of the laws of life, and of the best means for its preservation, live in larger houses, with freer ventilation, and upon food better adapted to support health and life. Their means of obtaining greater comforts and more luxuries, are to them, though perhaps unconsciously, the very reason of their prolonged lives, besides this, they are less harassed by the fears and uncertainty of obtaining for themselves and families a sufficiency of food and clothing. They are thus relieved of some of the most depressing influences, which tend to reduce the energy of mind and body in the poor, and render the latter more susceptible to the inroads of disease.

    Sanitary regulations affect the pauper class of the population more directly than any other, because they live in situations and circumstances which expose them more to attacks of disease. They are more crowded, they live more in cellars, their apartments are less ventilated, and more exposed to vapors and other emanations, &c., hence ventilation, sewerage, and all other sanitary regulations, are more necessary for them and would produce a greater comparative change in their condition. The influence of drainage upon the health and lives of the population, is too well known to require, at this day, any argument. . . .

    The Annual Reports of the City Inspector show that nearly one-half the deaths by consumption are of the foreign part of the population, and that more than one-third the whole number of deaths are of foreigners. Such an immense disproportion can only be accounted for on the supposition that some extraordinary causes of death prevail among the strangers who come to reside among us. Now it is pretty well ascertained fact, that a large majority of the cellar and court population of this city consists of persons of foreign birth and their children. Of the Dispensary patients, about 60 per cent. are natives of other countries, and if it were possible to ascertain the parentage of the children receiving aid from these institutions, we should find a larger proportion than this directly dependent upon foreigners. There is no doubt that 75 per cent. of them are either immigrants, or the children of such. Put these facts, then, side by side, and we are confirmed in the conclusion that the domiciliary condition of these poor beings, the confined spaces in which they dwell, the unwholesome air they breathe, and their filth and degradation, are prolific sources of an immense amount of distress and sickness, which in their turn, serve, by the loss of time, of wages, and of strength, to aggravate the miserableness of their condition, to increase the danger to the public health, and the burden of public and private charity.

    The evils thus resulting are occasionally exhibited in an endemic form, i.e., some disease of a marked character will break out and attack a considerable number of persons in the same neighborhood, the extent of its prevalence depending upon the extent of the cause, or the facilities for its propagation. Thus a fever may commence in a certain place inhabited mostly by the destitute and filthy: -- if the adjoining tenements are occupied by the same class of persons, and kept in the same dirty and ill-ventilated condition, the tenants of the latter will be very liable to attacks of the same disorder. The disease will often be observed to pass by houses in a better condition, and re-appear at a distance, where similar causes prevail. . . .

THE AMENDED CHARTER OF 1849

On April 3, 1849, the City Charter of New York was amended in several important ways, the most decisive of which, was the lengthening of the mayor's term from one year to two. A portion of the amended charter follows.

(Source: The Amended Charter of the City of New York, April 13, 1849.)

. . . SEC. 26. The first election of officers to be elected under this act, shall be held at the next general state election. The mayor, who shall be elected at the charter election, on the second Tuesday in April, one thousand eight hundred and forty-nine, shall hold his office until the first Monday of January, one thousand eight hundred and fifty-one, and the aldermen and assistant aldermen who shall be elected at that election, shall hold their offices until the first Monday of January, one thousand eight hundred and fifty, and no longer. All officers of said city government, who shall be in office when this act shall take effect, shall hold their offices and execute the duties thereof, until their successors shall be duly qualified.

SEC. 27. The seventh section of the act entitled "an act to amend the charter of the City of New York," passed April 7th, 1830, and all provisions of law and of charter, which are inconsistent with this act, are hereby repealed.

SEC. 28. All such parts of the charter of the city of New York, and the several acts of the legislature amending the same, or in any manner affecting the same, as are inconsistent with this act, are hereby repealed; but so much and such parts thereof as are not inconsistent with the provisions of this law, shall not be construed as repealed, altered or modified, or in any form affected thereby, but shall continue and remain in full force and virtue.

SEC. 29. This act shall be submitted for the approval of the electors of the city and county of New York, at an election to be held in said city, on the second Tuesday of April, one thousand eight hundred and forty-nine, for which the common council of the city shall make the necessary arrangements. The tickets which shall be polled at the said election, shall contain either the words "in favor of amendments to charter," or "against amendments to charter," and if a majority of all the persons voting thereon at the same time and at the same election, shall vote the ticket, "in favor of amendments to charter," this act shall become a law; if a majority of such persons shall vote "against amendments to charter," this act shall be void. . . .

THE IMMIGRANTS OF NEW YORK - 1850's

From its earliest days, New York has been the primary city for the entry of European immigrants to the United States. The following selection describes one of the many immigrant enclaves established in the city during the nineteenth century.

(Source: Karl Theodor Griesinger, Land und Leute in America: Skizzen aus dem Amerikanischen Leben, 2 vols., Stuttgart, 1863.)

The traveller who passes up Broadway, through Chatham Street, into the Bowery, up Houston Street, and thence right to First Avenue will find himself in a section which has very little in common with the other parts of New York. The arrangement of the streets and the monotony of the brownstone dwellings are similar, but the height and detail of the houses, the inhabitants, and their language and customs differ greatly from those of the rest of New York. This is "Kleindeutschland," or "Deutschlandle," as the Germans call this part of the city. . . .

Life in Kleindeutschland is almost the same as in the Old Country. Bakers, butchers, druggists-all are Germans. There is not a single business which is not run by Germans. Not only the shoemakers, tailors, barbers, physicians, grocers, and innkeepers are German, but the pastors and priests as well. There is even a German lending library where one can get all kinds of German books. The resident of Kleindeutschland need not even know English in order to make a living, which is a considerable attraction to the immigrant.

The shabby apartments are the only reminder that one is in America. Tailors or shoemakers use their living rooms as workshops, and there is scarcely space to move about. The smell in the house is not too pleasant, either, because the bedrooms ahve no windows, and there is a penetrating odor of sauerkraut. But the Germans do not care. They look forward to the time when they can afford a three-room apartment; and they would never willingly leave their beloved Kleindeutschland. The Americans who own all these buildings know this. That's why they do not consider improving the housing conditions. They like the Germans as tenants because they pay their rent, punctually, in advance, and keep the buildings neat and clean. The landlords are interested in keeping the German tenants crowded together because such buildings bring more profit than one-story houses.
. . . Deutschlandle certainly deserves its name, because 15,000 German families, comprising seventy to seventy-five thousand people live here. New York has about 120,000 German born inhabitants. Two-thirds of these live in Kleindeutschland. They come from every part of Germany, although

those from northern Germany are rarer than those from the southern part, and Hessians people from Baden, Wuertembergers, and Rhenish Bavarians are most numerous. . . .

On Sunday the movement in the streets is like that in a dovecote. People go from the inn to the church and back to the inn again. Everybody wears his Sunday clothes and is in high spirits. In the afternoon, on days when the weather is good, almost everybody leaves town and goes on a picnic. On Sunday night there is still more merriment in Kleindeutschland. The inns are crowded, even with women. There is music, in spite of the laws against making noise on Sunday.

The Germans have a Volkstheater, although the name theatre can hardly be applied to this long hall where the consumption of beer and cheese is a major activity. At the end of the hall is a small stage; and the performances are not realy plays as much as entertainment by comedians whom the proprietor hires to amuse his customers. Their ribald songs receive the enthusiastic applause of the audience. The people enjoy themselves immensely; the entertainment costs only ten cents, and one gets a free beer now and then. Such is the way Sunday is celebrated in Kleindeutschland. . . .

FERNANDO WOOD PROPOSES SECESSION - 1861

When, after Abraham Lincoln's election, it seemed certain that the Southern states would secede from the United States, Mayor Fernando Wood proposed to the Common Council that New York City secede from the United States and establish Manhattan as a free and independent city, so as to carry on trade and business with both North and South. Part of this extraordinary message follows.

(Source: Documents of the Board of Aldermen, XXVIII, no. I, New York, 1861.)

TO THE HONORABLE THE COMMON COUNCIL:
GENTLEMEN:

We are entering upon the public duties of the year, under circumstances as unprecedented as they are gloomy and painful to contemplate. The great trading and producing interests of not only the city of New York, but of the entire country, are prostrated by a monetary crisis; and though similar calamities have before befallen us, it is the first time that they have emanated from causes having not other origin than that which may be traced to political disturbances. . . .

It would seem that a dissolution of the Federal Union is inevitable. Having been formed originally upon a basis of general and mutual protection, but separate local independence, each State reserving the entire and absolute control of its own domestic affairs, it is evidently impossible to keep them together, longer than they deem themselves fairly treated by each other, or longer than the interests, honor, and fraternity of the people of the several States are satisfied. Being a government created by opinion, its continuance is dependent upon the continuance of the sentiment which form formed it. It cannot be preserved by coercion or held together by force. A resort to this last dreadful alternative would of itself destroy not only the government, but the lives and property of the people.

If these forebodings shall be realized, and a separation of the States shall occur, momentous considerations will be presented to the corporate authorities of this city. We must provide for the new relations which sill necessarily grow out of the new condition of public affairs. . . .

Being the child of the Union -- having drawn our sustenance from its bosom, and arisen to our present power and strength through the vigor of our mother -- when deprived of her maternal advantages, we must rely upon our own resources, and assume a position predicated upon the new phase which public affairs will present, and upon the inherent strength which our geographical, commercial, political, and financial preeminence imparts to us.

With our aggrieved brethren of the Slave States we have friendly relations and a common sympathy....Our ships have penetrated to every clime, and so have New York capital, energy, and enterprise found their way to almost every county and town of the American Union. If we have derived sustenance from the Union, so have we, in return, disseminated blessings for the common benefit of all. Therefore, New York has a right to expect, and should endeavor to preserve, a continuance of uninterrupted intercourse with every section....

Much no doubt can be said in favor of the justice and policy of a separation. It may be said that secession or revolution in any of the United States would be a subversion of all Federal authority, and, so far as the Central Government is concerned, the resolving of the community into its original elements -- that if part of the States form new combinations and governments, other states may do the same. California and her sisters of the Pacific will no doubt set up an independent republic, and husband their own rich mineral resources. The Western States, equally rich in cereals and other agricultural products, will probably do the same. Then it may be said -- Why should not New York City, instead of supporting by her contributions in revenue two thirds of the expenses of the United States, become also equally independent? As a free city, with but a nominal duty on imports, her local government could be supported without taxation upon her people. Thus we could live free from taxes, and have cheap goods nearly duty free. In this she would have the whole and united support of the Southern States, as well as of all other States to whose interests and rights under the Constitution she has always been true.

It is well for individuals or communities to look every danger square in the face, and to meet it calmly and bravely....If the Confederacy is broken up, the Government is dissolved; and it behooves every distinct community, as well as every individual, to take care of themselves.

When disunion has become a fixed and certain fact, why may not New York disrupt the bands which bind her to a venal and corrupt master -- to a people and a party that have plundered her revenues, attempted to ruin her commerce, taken away the power of self-government, and destroyed the Confederacy of which she was the proud Empire City? Amid the gloom which the present and prospective condition of things must cast over the country, New York, as a Free City, may shed the only light and hope for a future reconstruction of our once blessed Confederacy.

Yet I am not prepared to recommend the violence implied in these views. In stating this arbument in favor of freedom, 'peaceably, if we can; forcibly, if we must,' let me not be misunderstood. The redress can be found only in appeals to the magnanimity of the people of the whole state. The events of the past two months have no doubt effected a change in the popular sentiment of the State on national politics. This change may bring us the desired relief, and thus we may be able to obtain a repeal of the laws to which I have referred, and a consequent restoration of our corporate rights.

FERNANDO WOOD,
Mayor.

THE METROPOLITAN FIRE DEPARTMENT - 1865

On March 30, 1865, the Common Council abolished the old voluntary fire companies, and created a new Metropolitan Fire District and Department. The following selection is a portion of this act, dealing with the rules and regulations of this new city department.

(Source: <u>The Laws of 1865 for the City of New York</u>, The Metropolitan Fire Department, New York, 1865.)

RULES AND REGULATIONS
of the
METROPOLITAN FIRE DEPARTMENT
- - - -

SEC. 1. The whole number of officers and members, to compose each Steam Fire-Engine and Hook and Ladder Company drawn by horses, is hereby fixed at twelve, as follows: Engine Companies -- one Foreman, one Assistant Foreman, one Engineer of steamer, one Stoker, one Driver, and seven Firemen. Hook and Ladder Companies -- One Foreman, one Assistant Foreman, one Dirver, and nine Firemen.

The pay of the force is hereby fixed as follows -- per annum: Chief Engineer, $3,000; Assistant, $2,000; District Engineers, $1,500; Foremen, $1,100; Assistant Foremen, $900; Engineers of steamers, $1,080; Stokers, Drivers, and Firemen, each $840; Superintendent of Telegraph, $1,800; Telegraph Operators, each $1,000; Battery Boy, $500; Lineman, $1,000; Bell-ringers, each $800.

UNIFORM.

§2. Uniform of the Commissioners, officers, and members of the Metropolitan Fire Department:

COMMISSIONERS

A blue cloth cap (navy style). A frock-coat made of navy-blue cloth, double-breasted, to button up close to the neck, with seven department regulation buttons of bronze metal on each breast, three on each skirt behind, and four on each sleeve at the cuff. A single-breasted vest made of the same material as coat, without collar, and eight regulation buttons. Pantaloons made of the same material as the coat. Skrtout overcoats made of navy-blue pilot cloth, double-breasted, to button up close to the neck, with seven regulation buttons on each breast, three on each skirt behind, and four on each sleeve at the cuff.

CHIEF ENGINEER.

That of the Chief Engineer shall be a red flannel shirt, made double-breasted, with rolling collar; dark blue pilot-cloth fire coat, in length to reach to and not below the knee, with pantaloons of the same material; white fire-cap, of the present New York cone style, with gilt front, and a device upon it of a steam fire-engine, with the word "Chief" in the arch above, and the initials of the wearer under; the device and lettering to be in black.

ASSISTANT AND DISTRICT ENGINEERS.

The Assistant Engineer shall be uniformed in all respects same as the Chief Engineer, except substituting the word "Assistant" for Chief upon the cap front; the District Engineers shall also be the same in every respect as the Chief and Assistant Engineer, except the cap front, the word "Engineer" only being placed in the arch above the device.

The fatigue-cap shall be made of fine navy-blue cloth, eight-inch top, band one and one-half inch wide, quarters one and one-half inch high, front of solid patent leather bound, two and one-half inches wide at centre, chin-straps one-half inch wide with metal slides, lining of leather, to be sewed into the seam at top, and band welt in the top, and one in the bottom of the band. The device to be the words Chief, Assistant, or Engineer, as on the fire-cap, in block letters in a semicircle; letters "M.F.D." in Old English, under the title, to be embroidered in gold bullion, and placed in the centre of the front of the cap.

OFFICERS AND MEMBERS OF ENGINE COMPANIES.

The uniform of the Foreman and Assistant of Engine Companies shall consist of a dark bluee flannel shirt, double-breasted, with rolling collar; dark blue pilot-cloth fire coat, in length to reach to and not below the knee, with pants of the same material; black fire-caps of the present New York style, with white stitched fronts, and black letters; the letters "M.F.D." in the arch of the front, with the title of their position immediately underneath on a straight line, the number of the company to which they are attached in the centre, and the initials of the wearer at the bottom. That of Engineer of steamer, Stoker, and Driver, shall be the same in every respect, excepting the color of the cap front, which shall be on a black ground, and the letters in white. The Firemen's uniform shall be the same in all respects as the Engineer of steamer, Stoker, and Driver, excepting the title of their position shall be omitted.

OFFICERS AND MEMBERS OF HOOK AND LADDER COMPANIES.

The uniform of officers and members of Hook and Ladder Companies shall be the same in all respects as those of Engine Companies, excepting the cap front, the addition to which shall be a device of a hook and ladder crossed. The Driver's front shall be of a red ground, with white letters, lettered in the same manner as those of Engine Companies; the Firemen's fronts shall be of a red ground, with black letters.

The fatigue-cap shall be made of navy-blue cloth, eight-inch top, band one and a half inches wide, quarters one and a half inches high, front of solid patent leather bound, one and thre-quarters inches wide at centre, with small white-metal slide, two chin-strap white-metal buttons, same as those worn upon the sleeve of the coat, and to be furnished in the same manner; lining of leather, to be sewed into the seam at top, and band welt in the top, and one in the bottom of the band. The device, a white-metal Maltese cross, with the appropriate emblems of the Department in the centre, the letters "M. F. D." and the number (numerically) on the points, and placed in the centre of the front of the cap.

SUMMER UNIFORM COAT.

The summer uniform coat of the officers and members of the Department shall be a sack coat made from dark blue flannel, without lining, short rolling collar, and no binding, three regulation buttons on breast and two on each sleeve, medium length, reaching to the end of the fingers when the arm is straight.

REGULATION BUTTONS.

For the Chief, Assistant Engineer, and Engineer, officers and members of the force, white-metal buttons shall be furnished by the Department to each memb er of the force, and worn by them while in its employ, and for which a receipt shall be given at the time of delivery. The device upon the button is hereby designated to be the letters M. F. D., within a wreath. There shall be worn upon each breast of the coat five buttons, three on each side of the skirt behind, and three on each sleeve at the cuff.

DUTIES OF THE CHIEF, ASSISTANT, AND DISTRICT ENGINEERS.

§ 3. The Chief, Assistant Engineer, and District Engineers, the officers and members of the several Fire Companies composing the Metropolitan Fire Department, shall devote their entire time to the interests of the Department.

§ 4. The Chief Engineer shall have and exercise supreme command at all fires over the Engineers, officers,and members of the Department. He shall have charge of all supplies, and issue them to companies under direction of the board. He shall locate all apparatus, and make a report thereof to the Board. He shall make a daily r eport of the number of men on duty and the condition of the several houses, apparatus, hose, horses, and harness, and see that proper discipline be observed by the officers and men; and his report shall state the supplies needed by each company under his command.

§ 5. The Assistant Engineer shall attend all fires in districts in which the Chief Engineer shall direct him to perform duty, and, in the absence of the Chief, shall perform the duties prescribed for that officer. He shall, under the Chief Engineer, act as superintendent of all mechanical business of the repair-shop and yard, and of the construction and repair of all apparatus ordered by the Board.

§ 6. The District Engineers, in the absence of the Chief and Assistant Engineer, shall have command at all fires occurring within the limits of such districts as the Chief may prescribe to each. They shall perform duty as Engineers in such sections as the Chief may designate, and in all districts other than their own shall act as subordinate to the Engineer of the district. They shall superintend all alterations or repairs to the houses of companies in their districts, and shall visit the same daily, and make a written report thereon to the Chief Engineer. They shall also make a monthly report to the Chief Engineer of all fires attended by them, and any violation of the rules of the Department, or disobedience of orders, by officers or members of the force. . . .

FIREMEN.

§ 12. The members shall keep their houses and bedding clean and in good order; they shall accompany their apparatus going to or returning from a fire, and when on duty at a fire, and not otherwise directed by the officer in command, shall remain by their apparatus. The Foreman shall cause to be kept by the officers and members of the force (serving in rotation as they stand on the roll) a proper and efficient watch day and night, so that at all times two men shall be on patrol in the neighborhood of the Engine or Hook and Ladder house, and one on watch in the house. Members doing such patrol duty shall report at the house hourly until relieved.

MISCELLANEOUS.

§ 13. Racing to or from fires is prohibited; and if the apparatus of the several companies proceed on the same street or avenue to or from a fire, they shall do so in single file.

§ 14. Crossing a line of hose when in use by a steam fire-engine is, unless in cases of the most absolute necessity, strictly prohibited.

§ 15. The officer in command shall precede his apparatus in going to or from a fire.

§ 16. No officer or member of the force shall appear on duty except he be properly clothed in the uniform prescribed for the Department; nor shall any officer or member of a Fire Company appear at a fire without his fire-cap.

§ 17. No spiritous or intoxicating liquors shall be allowed on the premises of any Metropolitan Fire Company, nor shall any game of chance be permitted thereon.

§ 18. No officer or member shall use profane, immoral, or indecent language in or about any Engine or Hook and Ladder house, or while at, going to, or returning from a fire; nor shall any officer or member visit places where intoxicating liquors are sold while in the uniform of this Department.

§ 19. Officers of companies, after a fire, having hose which does not belong to them, shall reutrn the same to the company to whom it belongs.

§ 20. The Driver, Engineer, and Stoker may ride on the engine, and the driver and one man on the tender, in going to or returning from fires, and no more; and the officer in command will be held responsible for a violation of this rule.

§ 21. Ingress and egress to and from fires, through the police lines, shall be made as near the centre of the street as practicable.

§ 22. No officer or member shall be entitled to pay for less than fifteen days' service. All appointments shall, so far as practicable, be made to date from the first or fifteenth of each month, and any member desiring to resign shall give written notice thereof at least five days previous to the time of such intended resignation. . . .

THE CHARTER OF 1870

On April 5, 1870, the Charter of 1870 was passed by the State Legislature. It was known as the so-called "Tweed Charter," for it gave William Marcy Tweed complete power over the city.

(Source: The Charter of 1870, April 5, 1870, found in <u>Manual of the Corporation of New York, 1870.</u>)

ARTICLE FIRST.
THE CORPORATE POWER.

Section 1. The corporation now existing and known by the name of "The Mayor, Council and Commonalty of the City of New York," shall continue to be a body politic and operate in fact and in name, by the same name, and shall have perpetual succession with all the grants, powers, and privileges heretofore held by the Mayor, Aldermen, and Commonalty of the city of New York, and not modified or repealed by the provisions hereinafter made by this act.

ARTICLE SECOND.
OF LEGISLATIVE POWER.

Sec. 2. The legislative power of the said corporation shall continue to be vested in a Board of Aldermen, and a Board of Assistant Aldermen, who together shall form the Common Council of the city of New York.

Sec. 3. The Board of Aldermen shall consist of fifteen members, to be elected upon a general ticket from the city at large.

Sec. 4. The Board of Assistant Aldermen shall consist of one Assistant Alderman to be decided in such assembly district.

Sec. 5. Such Aldermen and Assistant Aldermen shall be elected as hereinafter proclaimed.

Sec. 6. The first election for Aldermen and Assistant Aldermen shall take place at a special election to be held in the city and county of New York, on the third Tuesday in May in the year eighteen hundred and seventy, and the Aldermen and Assistant Aldermen then elected shall take office on the first Monday in June following, at noon, and shall supercede the Common Council now in office, whose terms of office shall then end. The Aldermen and Assistant Aldermen so elected in May, eighteen hundred and seventy shall hold office until the first Monday in January, which will be in the year eighteen hundred and seventy-two. There shall be Aldermen and Assistant Aldermen elected at the general election in November, eighteen hundred and seventy-one, and annually thereafter at every succeeding general election, who shall take office at noon on the first Monday of January in each and every year following their election. All the provisions of the ruling to the judicial election to be held in May, eighteen hundred and seventy, in as they are applicable, shall apply to the first election under this act for such Aldermen and Assistant Aldermen; and all the provisions of law relating to general elections in the city of New York, so far as they are applicable in respect to the manner of conducting elections and the canvass and estimate of votes, shall apply to each succeeding election for Aldermen and Assistant Aldermen.

Sec. 7. Each Board of the Common Council shall have power to direct a special election to be held to supply the place of any member whose seat shall become vacant and the person elected to supply such vacancy shall hold his seat for the remainder of the term of his immediate predecessor.

Sec. 8. The Boards shall meet in separate chambers, and a majority of each shall be a quorum.

Sec. 9. Each Board shall
1. Choose a president from its own members.
2. Appoint a clerk and other officers.
3. Determine the rules of its own proceedings.
4. Be the judge of the returns of election, and the right of election and qualifications of its own members.
5. Keep a journal of its proceedings.
6. Sit with open doors, except when the public welfare shall require secrecy; and
7. Shall have authority to compel the attendance of absent members and to punish its members for disorderly behavior; and to expel a member with the concurrence of two-thirds of the members elected to the Board.

Sec. 10. Every member expelled from either Board shall thereby forfeit all his rights and power as an Alderman or Assistant Alderman.

Sec. 11. The stated and occasional meetings of each Board shall be regulated by its own resolutions and rules, and both Boards may meet at the same time, or different days, as they may severally judge expedient.

Sec. 12. Every legislative act of the Common Council shall be by resolution or ordinance, and every ordinance or joint resolution shall, before it shall take effect be presented, duly certified, to the Mayor for his approval.

Sec. 13. The Mayor shall return such ordinance or resolution to the board from which it originated, within ten days after receiving it, or at the next meeting of such board.

Sec. 14. If he approve it, he shall sign it. If he disapprove, he shall specify his objections thereto. If he do not return it with such disapproval within the time above specified, it shall take effect as if he had approved it.

Sec. 15. Such objections of the Mayor shall be entered at large on the journal of the board to which they are sent.

Sec. 16. The board to which such ordinance or resolution shall have been returned with objections, shall, after the expiration of not less than ten days thereafter, proceed to reconsider the same, and if, on reconsideration, it shall pass both boards by a vote of at least three-fourths of all the members elected to each board, it shall take effect. In all such cases the votes shall be taken by ayes and noes, and the names of all persons voting for or against its passage on such reconsideration shall be entered on the journal of each board.

Sec. 17. No ordinance or resolution shall be valid unless it shall receive the assent of both boards within the term fixed by law to such boards.

Sec. 18. Any ordinance or resolution may originate in either board, and when it shall have passed one board may be rejected or amended in the other; but no ordinance or resolution shall be passed except by a vote of the majority of all the members elected to each board. But in case any ordinance or resolution involves the expenditure of money, the votes of three-fourths of all the members elected to each board shall become necessary to its passage. No money shall be expended for any celebration, procession or entertainment of any kind, or on any occasion, unless by the votes of four-fifths of all the members elected to each board. No additional allowance beyond the original claim which exists under any contract with the Corporation, or for any services on its account, or in its employment, shall ever be passed by the Common Council, except by the unanimous vote thereof.

Sec. 19. The clerk of the Board of Aldermen shall, by virtue of his office, be clerk of the Common Council, and shall perform all the duties heretofore performed by the clerk of the Common Council, except such as shall be assigned to the clerk of the Board of Assistant Aldermen; and it shall be his duty to keep open for inspection, at all reasonable times, the records and minutes of the proceedings of the Common Council, except such as shall be specially ordered otherwise. The clerk of each board shall appoint and remove at pleasure deputy clerks in his department, not to exceed the number now authorized by law or ordinance. The clerk of the Common Council shall keep the seal of the city; and his signature shall be necessary to all leases, grants, and other documents, as under existing laws.

Sec. 20. It shall be the duty of the clerks of the respective boards to publish all resolutions and ordinances and amendments thereof which shall be introduced or passed, and also the final proceedings, except such parts as may require secrecy; and no vote shall be taken in either board upon the passage of a resolution or an ordinance which shall contemplate any specific improvement, or involve the sale, disposition, or appropriation of public property, or the expenditure of public moneys or income therefrom, or by any tax or assessment, until after such notice shall have been published at least three days; and whenever any vote shall be taken, such resolution or ordinance shall, before the same shall be sent to the other board, or to the Mayor, and immediately after the adjournment of the board at which the same shall have been passed, be published with the yeas and nays, and with the names of the persons voting for and against the same, as part of the proceedings; and no resolution or ordinance which shall have passed the board shall be acted upon by the other board on the same day.

Sec. 21. The Common Council shall have power to make, continue, modify, and repeal such ordinances, regulations, and resolutions as may be necessary to carry into effect any and all of the powers now vested in, or by this act conferred upon, the Corporation, and shall have power to enforce obedience thereto and observance thereof, by ordaining penalties for each and every violation thereof, in such sums as it may deem expedient, not exceeding one hundred dollars. And shall have power to make such ordinances and with such penalties, in the matters and for the purposes following, in addition to other powers elsewhere specially granted, viz:

1. To regulate traffic and sales in the streets, highways, roads, and public places.

2. To regulate the use of the streets, highways, roads, and public places by foot passengers, vehicles, railways, and locomotives.

3. To regulate the use of sidewalks, building-fronts, and house-fronts within the street lines.

4. To prevent and remove encroachments upon and obstructions to the streets, highways, roads, and public places.

5. To regulate the opening of street surfaces, the laying of gas or water mains, the installing and repairing of sewers, and erecting gas-lights.

6. To provide for and regulate the opening, widening, and extending of streets below Fourteenth Street.

7. To regulate the numbering of the houses and lots in the streets and avenues, and the naming of the streets, avenues, and public places.

8. To regulate and prevent the throwing or depositing of ashes, offal, dirt, or garbage in the streets.

9. To regulate the cleaning of the streets side-walks, and gutters, and removing ice, hail, and snow from them.

10. To regulate the use of the streets and sidewalks, for signs, sign-posts, awnings, awning posts, and horse-troughs.

11. To provide for an regulate street pavements, cross-walks, curb-stones, gutter-stones, and sidewalks.

12. To regulate public cries, advertising-noises, and ringing bells in the streets.

13. In regard to the relation between all the officers and employes of the Corporation in respect to each other, the Corporation, and the people.

14. In relation to street beggars, vagrants, and mendicants.

15. In relation to the use of guns, pistols, fire-arms, fire-crackers, fire-works, and detonating works of all descriptions within the city.

16. In relation to intoxication, fighting, and quarrelling in the streets.

17. In relation to places of public amusement.

18. In relation to exhibiting or carrying banners, placards, or flags in or across the streets or from houses.

19. In relation to the exhibition of advertisements or hand-bills along

the streets.

20. In relation to the construction, repairs, and use of vaults, cisterns, areas, hydrants, pumps, and sewers.

21. In relation to partition fences and walls.

22. In relation to the construction, repair, care, and use of markets, [docks, wharves, piers, and slips.]

23. In relation to the licensing and business of public cartmen, truckmen, hackmen, cabmen, expressmen, boatmen, pawnbrokers, junkdealers, hawkers, pedlers, and venders.

24. In relation to the inspection and sealing of weights and measures, and enforcing the keeping and use of proper weights and measures by venders.

25. In relation to the inspection, weighing, and measuring of firewood, coal, hay, and straw, and the cartage of the same.

26. In relation to the mode and manner of suing for, collecting and disposing of the penalties provided for a violation of all ordinances.

27. And for carrying into effect and enforcing any of the powers, privileges, and rights at any time granted and bestowed upon or possessed by the said Corporation.

Sec. 22. The Common Council shall have no power to impose taxes or assessments, or borrow money, or contract debts, or loan the credit of the city, unless specially authorized so to do by act of the Legislature, and all the legislative power of the city shall be subordinate to and be exercised in conformity with such special grants, restrictions, or limitations as are now or hereafter may be prescribed by the Legislature.

ARTICLE THIRD.
OF THE EXECUTIVE POWER.

Sec. 23. The executive power of the Corporation shall be vested in the Mayor and the departments herein created.

Sec. 24. The Mayor shall be the chief executive officer of the Corporation; shall be elected at a general election, and hold his office for the term of two years, commencing on the first day of January next after his election. The first election for Mayor shall be at the general election in November, in the year eighteen hundred and seventy.

Sec. 25. Whenever the Mayor shall be under impeachment, or there shall be a vacancy in the office of the Mayor, or whenever by sickness, absence from the city, or other cause, he shall be prevented from attending to the duties of his office, the President of the Board of Aldermen shall act as Mayor, and possess all the rights and powers of Mayor, except as hereinafter provided in regard to appointments to office during such disability, or, in case of a vacancy, until the next general elections. . . .

THE TWEED RING - 1871

New York City politics have often been characterized as blatantly corrupt. The most striking example of New York's political corruption was the notorious Tweed Ring led by William Marcy Tweed. However, the excesses of Tweed's rule, eventually led New Yorkers to revolt against his autocratic and corrupt domination of the city. What follows is a portion of an article describing the proceedings of a great protest meeting held in New York in opposition to "Boss" Tweed and his cohorts.

(Source: New York Times, April 7, 1871.)

The large hall of Cooper Institute was filled to overflowing last evening with an audience composed of the most respectable and influential of our citizens of both political parties, who had assembled to indorse the views expressed by prominent mumbers of the Bar and other professions, in relation to the measures now before the Legislature, which are intended to still further engulf the City in debt and the degradation of political corruption. Among the prominent gentlemen on the stage and in the audience were Calvin T. Hulburd, Charles Butler, Henry Clews, James M. Brown, William Tracey, John D. Jones, William H. Aspinwall, J. H. Gauller, John J. McCandless, Charles Abernethy, R. H. McCurdy, Isaac H. Bailey, Samuel J. Glassey, El L. Fancher, Henry Nicoll, Henry Grinnell, Ambrose C. Kingsland, Thomas E. Clerke, and others. The meeting was very enthusiastic,and the speeches were frequently and liberally applauded. It was called to order by Hon. WM. E. DODGE who spoke as follows:

In view of the alarming aspects of public affairs generally, and particularly of the introduction into the Legislature of this State of several measures disastrously affecting, as we believe, the material and political, and especially the moral and educational interests of this City, the New York City Council of Political Reform has directed the undersigned, the Executive Committee of the Council, to call a meeting of such of our fellow citizens as are opposed to these measures, to make public protest against them.

The most important of the measures referred to are the New York City Tax bill, Senate bill No. 30, nominally for the establishment of parochial schools, the bill for the abolition of the Board of Education, the bill to repeal the law regulating public amusements, and the bill for modifying the present Registry law.

Mr. DODGE concluded by nominating the following Executive Committee:

Hon. Geo. C. Barrett,	Robert Hoe,
W. Walter Phelps,	Dexter A. Hawkins,
Hon. W. F. Havemeyer,	S. D. Moulton,
James M. Halsted,	E. B. Wesley,
George P. Putman,	S. S. Constant,
A. R. Wetmore,	A. C. Post, M.D.,
W. H. Neilson,	Hon. John Wheeler,
Thomas C. Acton,	John Stephenson,
John P. Crosby,	

He then nominated for presiding officer Hon. WM. F. HAVEMEYER, Ex-Mayor, who in a few remarks thanked the audience for the honor conferred in electing him as their Chairman, expressed his sympathy with the cause which had brought them together, and hoped that the movement would result in great good to the City and those who were engaged in the labor of reform. . . .

Resolved, That the neglect by the friends of good government of their inherent duties as citizens of a Republic, and their having the management of political affairs and the control of the local and State Governments in the hands of idlers and adventurers, is one of the saddest evidences of a decline in public virtue, and that we call upon all good citizens to make their power felt by uniting to demand from the political parties with which they are accustomed to act, that they shall, as a condition of continued support, present candidates for office who are morally and intellectually qualified, and who understand, and will defend, the fundamental principles of our institutions.

Resolved, That, as individual patriotism, however earnest, cannot cope with the organized bands who, under mere party guise, seize upon the organs of government, we regard the Council of Political Reform, which has for its object the union of all friends of good government, without regard to the views which they entertain upon the national questions which divide parties, as worthy of the approval of all good citizens, and we call upon them to give it their active co-operation and support.

The Chairman then introduced Hon. WM. M. EVARTS, who spoke as follows:

FELLOW-CITIZENS: I am quite sure that if the patriotic laborous efforts of the Council of Political Reform now carried on for some years, not only in this City, but in this State, laying the foundations for great and important public action, could be rewarded tonight by no consequences from their call, but this very assemblage itself, it would be to them evidence, to you evidence, to honest men evidence, to knaves evidence, that the people of this City and of this country do take an interest in the substantial welfare of the commonwealth and in the name and fame of American citizenship. Applause. For this meeting, so vast in its numbers, so universal in its comprehension of the interests and the pursuits of this community, so earnest and honest in its make-up, is brought hither by none of the excitements of politics, by none of the zeal for candidates, or by none of the Interest of the honest or more substantial in the results of election. The conjuration which has brought you together is to prove the conjuration that is to bind you in the warfare, whose weapons you to-night assume, and that is a conjuration as deep and as earnest as that with which the foundations of this Republic were raised, and with which it was saved from the ruin that was threatened it by violence. [Applause.] For of what good is it that we should have brave and heroic ancestors, and that we should have brave and heroic contemporaries on the field of battle, adequate to join issue with the strongest rebellion that the world has ever seen, if, when this heroism has secured a perfect triumph, our imbecility, our ignorance, our folly surrenders to the shrine of fraud what would not be yielded to the roar of battle! [Applause.] The truth is, gentlemen, that a meeting like this is but a symptom of what occupies the public mind throughout the whole country -- of deep, of serious concern about the very institutions upon which our liberty rests. Applause But the working force of this common and equal right without protector, without a guardian, except what each brave heart and each shrewd head shall furnish to each citizen, to wield the powers that free Government had given what headway, what strength this scattered and diffused force can have against powerful combinations stimulated by sordid purposes and confederated in the bond of common infamy. Now, gentlemen, this Council of Political Reform have undertaken to set on foot the sentiments, the movements, and facilitate the combinations by which disorganization, which is the hope, the plan, the strength of the combined movements of selfishness and fraud, finds its hopes shall cease, and it shall be known that if subterranean links can be made between the knaves of both parties, open and manly combinations can be made by the true men of both parties, and the hosts may be counted on one side and the other. [Applause.] The occasion of this meeting is the pendency of certain measures before the Legislature threatening serious accession to the strength against which we are allied, serious innovations of the common right of citizens; serious interference with the institutions of our liberty, civil and religious, in which we have our pride and our safety. And the situation is propitious. We stand not indifferent to parties; we are all adherents of one party or the another, but we mean that parties shall confine themselves to their true functions, which is honesty, usefully to maintain the principles on one side and the other for which and in which the party has its life, by which and through which, thus maintained and thus administered, the nation has its life; but when either party, especially the party to which we respectively adhere, loses its public virtue and first becomes a faction seeking only the selfish interests of its members, and the -- oh, sad catastrophe! -- a conspiracy seeking the public life; then our hands, our voices, our votes, are the first to be raised to crush the treason against the common safety. . . .

    Rev. Dr. BELLOWS was then introduced and said: I come forward to give my testimony in favor of the object of this meeting, and to say a word about the immense difficulty of governing this City. We have 517,000 living in tenement houses out of a population of 740,000; we have 30,000 professional thieves, more than 20,000 lewd women, and 3,000 grog-shops, besides 2,000 gambling establishments. We have an immense foreign population, but nothing the worse for being foreign. We have of two nations alone 350,000 or 400,000 of whom 170,000 who profess the Roman Catholic religion may be considered as like a box of iron molded into a solid mass, and who govern the politics of this City. But what is to be done if the upper classes, representing the professional and educated class, is cowardly and negligent, and for one reason or another neglects its political duty! What is the legal profession -- so well represented by the chief speaker tonight -- doing to break down this odious ascendency? What are the common people to think if they see the educated classes shrinking from their duty? The lawyer, he said, may tell them that it was no concern of his to sacrifice the interests of his client to the interests of justice, but that was no valid plea. He did not want to trust rich men with opening streets in which they themselves had an interest: he would rather trust the opening to men who were not rich. He next alluded to the little done by the pulpit and by the stock brokers in Wall-street to purify the City Government. There was rottenness at the bottom and rottenness and cowardice at the top, and they wanted courage to speak the truth. They need not expect to have reform as long as these things lasted. His fears were not so much about those who occupied tenement-houses; he feared and dreaded most the cowardice and imbecility of those in the top places.

    The meeting was then adjourned by the Chairman, and the assemblage dispersed.

THE CHARTER OF 1873

Following the downfall of the Tweed Ring, the new City Council threw out the infamous Tweed Charter of 1870, and adopted a new one, part of which follows.

(Source: New York City Charter, An Act to Reorganize the Local Government, April 30, 1873.)

ARTICLE I.
The Corporate Powers.

Section 1. The corporation now existing and known by the name of "The Mayor, Aldermen, and Commonalty of the city of New York" shall continue to be a body politic and corporate, in fact and in name, by the same name, and have perpetual succession, with all the grants, powers and privileges heretofore held by the mayor, aldermen, and commonalty of the city of New York, and not modified or repealed by the provisions of this act.

ARTILCE II.
Of Legislative Powers.

Sec. 2. The legislative power of the said corporation shall continue to be vested in a board of aldermen and a board of assistant aldermen, who together shall form the common council of the city of New York. The board of assistant aldermen is hereby abolished from and after the first day of January, eighteen hundred and seventy-five; and from and after that date the board of aldermen is hereby declared to be the common council, and shall solely possess the powers and perform all the duties by law conferred or imposed upon the board of aldermen, and board of assistant aldermen, the common council, or any one or more of them.

Sec. 3. Such aldermen shall be elected as hereinafter provided.

Sec. 4. The board of aldermen now in office shall hold office until the first Monday of January, in the year eighteen hundred and seventy-five, the same being the term for which they were elected. There shall be twenty twenty-one aldermen elected at the general state election which shall occur in the year eighteen hundred and seventy-four, three of whom shall be elected in each senate district of the city, as now constituted, and shall be residents of the district in which they are elected, but no voter shall vote for more than two of said aldermen. There shall also be elected six aldermen at large, to be voted for on a separate ballot, but no voter shall vote for more than four of the said aldermen at large. The members of the board of aldermen shall hold office for the space of one year, and shall take office on the first Monday in January next succeeding their election, at noon. Annually thereafter, at the general state election, there shall be elected a full board of aldermen as hereinbefore provided.

[Amended by sec. 1, chap. 757, laws of 1873.] Any vacancy now existing, or which may hereafter occur, in either the board of aldermen, or board of assistant aldermen, by reason of the death, or resignation, or of any other cause, of a member of either of said boards, shall be filled by election by the board in which such vacancy exists or shall arise, by a vote of a majority of all the members elected to said board, and the person so elected to fill any such vacancy shall serve until the first day of January, at noon, next succeeding the first general election, occurring not less than thirty days after the happening of such vacancy, but not beyond the expiration of the term in which the vacancy shall occur, and at such election, a person shall be elected to serve the remainder, if any, of such unexpired term.

From and after the termination of the term of office of the board of assistant aldermen, as herein provided, the board of aldermen shall alone constitute the common council, and shall exercise the entire legislative powers of the said city. The aldermen shall from time of the passage of this act be the supervisors of the county of New York.

Sec. 5. The boards shall meet in separate chambers. . . .

CONSOLIDATION ACT OF THE LAWS OF 1882

In 1882, the State Legislature approved an act to consolidate into one charter all the laws of New York City that affected the public interest. The Charter of 1873 was fully incorporated into this act. An excerpt follows.

(Source: Laws Relating to the City of New York, 1882.)

CHAPTER I.
BOUNDARIES OF CITY AND COUNTY AND OF WARDS.

SECTION 1. The city and county of New York shall contain the islands called Manhattan Island, North Brother's Island, Great Barn or Ward's Island, Little Barn or Randall's Island, Manning's or Blackwell's Island, Nutten or Governor's Island, Bedloe's Island, Bucking or Ellis Island, and the Oyster Islands; and also all the territory which formerly constituted the towns of Morrisania, West Farms and Kingsbridge, in the county of Westchester, being all the territory which lies westerly of the centre of the Bronx river, and southerly of a line commencing in the centre of the Bronx river, at latitude forty degrees, fifty-three minutes, fifty-nine and twenty-three one-hundredths seconds north, and longitude seventy-three degrees, fifty-one minutes, thirty-five and sixty-seven one-hundredths seconds west of Greenwich, and running on a straight line westerly to a point on the low-water mark of the eastern bank of the Hudson river at latitude forty degrees, fifty-four minutes, fifty-three and twenty-one one-hundredths seconds north, and longitude seventy-three degrees, fity-four minutes, thirty-eight and sixty-four one-hundredths seconds west of Greenwich, and thence westerly in a straight line to the west bounds of the state; together with all the land under water within the following bounds: beginning at Spuyten Duyvil creek, where the low-water mark of the northern bank thereof intersects the low-water mark on the eastern bank of the Hudson river, and running thence along said creek at low-water mark on the northern side thereof to the Harlem river, thence along the low-water mark on the eastern bank thereof to the Bronx kills; thence along the low-water mark on the northern bank thereof to the low-water mark of the north-western shore of Long Island Sound, thence along the low-water mark of the north-western and northern shore of Long Island Sound to the mouth of the Bronx river at Hunt's point; thence along the low-water-mark as far as the same may extend in the Bronx river, and the mouth thereof to the low-water mark of Long Island Sound at the western side of Clauson's Point; thence across Long Island Sound to College Point on Nassau or Long Island to low-water mark there; thence south-westerly across Flushing bay to low-water-mark at Sanford's Point, between Flushing and Bowery bays, including Great Barn or Ward's Island, and Little Barn or Randall's Island; then along Nassau or Long Island shore, at low-water mark, and including Manning's or Blackwell's Island, to the south side of the Red Hook; then across the North river so as to include Nutten or Governor's Island, Bedloe's Island, Bucking or Ellis Island, and the Oyster Islands, to the west bounds of the state; and thence northerly along the west bounds of the state to the junction with the above-mentioned prolongation westerly of the northern boundary line of the city and county of New York, from the low-water mark on the eastern bank of the Hudson river; thence easterly along said line to the easterly bank of the Hudson river at low-water mark, to the point or place of beginning.

§2. The city of New York contains all that part of this state comprehended within the bounds of the county of New York, and is divided into twenty-four wards, in the manner following, that is to say:

The first ward shall begin in the middle of Broadway, at a point where it is intersected by the middle of Liberty street, and run from the said point of intersection, through the middle of Liberty street, south-easterly, to the middle of Maiden lane; then down the middle of Maiden lane, and from thence in a straight line running in the same direction across the East river, to low-water mark on Nassau or Long Island; and thence along Nassau or Long Island shore, at low water mark, to the south side of Red Hook; and then across Hudson River, so as to include Nutten or Governor's Island, Bedloe's Island, Bucking or Ellis Island and the Oyster Islands, and all the waters of this state in the bay of New York, and to the southward thereof, and which are not comprehended in any other county, to low-water mark on the west side of Hudson river, or so far as the bounds of this state extend; then up along the west side of Hudson river, at low-water mark, or along the limits of this state, to a place due west from the middle of the west end of Liberty street; then to the middle of Liberty street; then through the middle of Liberty street to the middle of Broadway, at the place of beginning.

§3. The second ward shall begin at the south-easterly corner of the first ward, and run thence along the easterly bounds thereof, across the East river to the middle of Broadway; then up the middle of Broadway to a point opposite the middle of Park row; then through the middle of Park row to a point opposite to the middle of Spruce (formerly George) street; then down the middle of Spruce street to the middle of Gold street; then through the middle of Gold street to a point opposite to the middle of Ferry street; then through the middle of Ferry street, in a line running in the same direction across the East river to Nassau or Long Island, to low-water mark; then along Nassau or Long Island, at low water, to the place of beginning.

§4. The third ward shall begin on the west side of Hudson river, at the north-westerly corner of the first ward, and running thence due east to the middle of Liberty street; then through the middle of Liberty street to the middle of Broadway; then through the middle of Broadway to a point opposite to the middle of Reade street; then through the middle of Reade street, in a line running in the same direction across Hudson river, to low-water mark, on the west side thereof, or so far as the bounds of the State extend; then down the west side of Hudson river, at low-water mark, or along the limits of this state, to the place of beginning.

§5. The fourth ward shall begin at the northerly corner of the second ward, and run thence through the middle of Chatham street to a point opposite to the middle of Catharine street; and then through the middle of Catharine street, in a line running in the same direction across the East river, to low-water mark, on Nassau or Long Island; then along Nassau or Long Island shore, at low-water mark, to the bounds of the second ward; and then north-westerly along the bounds of the second ward, to the place of beginning.

§6. The fifth ward shall begin at the north-westerly corner of the third ward, and run thence along the northerly bounds thereof, to the middle of Broadway; then through the middle of Broadway to the middle of Canal street; then through the middle of Canal street to Hudson river; then due west to low-water mark, on the west side of Hudson river, or so far as the bounds of this State extend; then down along the west side of Hudson river, at low water mark, or along the limits of this State, to the place of beginning.

§7. The sixth ward shall begin at a point in the middle of Broadway, where it is intersected by the middle of Canal street, and run thence through the middle of Anal street to where it is intersected by the middle of Centre street; then through the middle of Centre street to the middle of Walker street; then through the middle of Walker and Canal streets to the middle of the Bowery road; then through the middle of the Bowery road to the middle of Chatham street; then through the middle of Chatham street and Park row to the middle of Broadway, and then through the middle of Broadway to the place of beginning.

§8. The seventh ward shall begin at the south-easterly corner of the fourth ward, and run thence along the easterly boundary of the fourth ward to the middle of Division street; then through the middle of Division street to the middle of Grand street; then through the middle of Grand street, in a line running in the same direction across the East river, to low-water mark on Nassau or Long Island; then along Nassau or Long Island Shore, at low-water mark, to the place of beginning.

§9. The eighth ward shall begin at the north-westerly corner of the fifth ward, and run thence along the northerly bounds of the said ward through Canal street to the middle of Broadway; then through the middle of Broadway to a point opposite to the middle of Houston street; then through the middle of Houston street to a point opposite to the middle of West Houston street; then through the middle of West Houston street to Hudson river; then due west to low-water mark, on the west side of Hudson river, or so far as the limits of this State extend; then down along the west side of Hudson river, at low-water mark, or along the limits of this State, to the place of beginning.

§10. The ninth ward shall begin at the north-westerly corner of the eighth ward, and run thence along the northerly bounds of the said ward through the middle of West Houston street to the middle of Hancock street; thence northerly through the middle of Hancock street to the middle of Bleecker street; thence north-westerly through the middle of Bleecker street to the middle of Carmine street; thence north-easterly through the middle of Carmine street to the middle of Sixth avenue; thence northerly through the middle of Sixth avenue to the middle of West Fourteenth street; thence westerly through the middle of West Fourteenth street to Hudson river; then due west to low-water mark on the west side of Hudson river; or or so far as the limits of this State extend; then down along the west side of Hudson river, at low-water mark, or along the limits of this State, to the place of beginning.

§ 11. The tenth ward shall begin at a point in the middle of the Bowery road, opposite to the middle of Division street; then through the middle of Division street to the middle of Norfolk street; then through the middle of Norfolk street to the middle of Rivington street; then through the middle of Rivington street to the middle of the Bowery road; then through the middle of the Bowery road to the place of beginning.

§ 12. The eleventh ward shall begin at a point in the middle of Rivington street, where Clinton street intersects Rivington street; and run thence through the middle of Clinton street to the middle of avenue B, and then northerly through the middle of Avenue B to the middle of Fourteenth street; thence easterly through the middle of East Fourteenth street to the East river; and thence running across the East river to low-water mark on Long Island; then along Long Island shore, at low-water mark, to a point opposite the middle of the easterly end of Rivington street; then in a direct line across the East river through the middle of Rivington street to the place of beginning.

§ 13. The twelfth ward shall include all that part of the city and county of New York lying northerly of a line running through the middle of Eighty-sixth street from the East to the North river, and south and west of Harlem river and Spuyten Duyvel creek, but including Randall's and Ward's Islands.

§ 14. The thirteenth ward shall begin at the north-easterly corner of the seventh ward, and thence along the easterly and northerly line of the said ward through the middle of Grand and Division streets, to the middle of Norfolk street; thence through the middle of Norfolk street to where it is intersected by the middle of Rivington street; then through the middle of Rivington street in a line running in the same direction across the East river to low-water mark on Nassau Island; and then along the shore of said island, at low-water mark, to the place of beginning.

§ 15. The fourteenth ward shall begin at a point in the middle of the Bowery road, where it is intersected by the middle of Walker street; then through the middle of the Bowery road to a point opposite the middle of Hous Houston street, then through the middle of Houston street to where it is intersected by the middle of Broadway; thence through the middle of Broadway to where it is intersected by the middle of Canal street; and then through the middle of Canal, Centre, and Walker streets, begin along the northerly bounds of the sixth ward, to the place of beginning.

§16. The fifteenth ward shall begin at a point in the middle of Fourteenth street where the middle of Sixth avenue intersects the middle of Fourteenth street, and run thence southerly through the middle of Sixth avenue to the middle of Carmine street; thence south-westerly through the middle of Carmine street to the middle of Bleecker street; thence south-easterly through the middle of Bleecker street to the middle of Hancock street; thence southerly through the middle of Hancock street to the middle of Houston street; thence easterly through the middle of Houston street to the middle of the Bowery road; thence northerly along the middle of the Bowery road and the middle of Fourth avenue to the middle of Fourteenth street, and thence westerly along the middle of Fourteenth street to the place of beginning.

§17. The sixteenth ward shall begin at the north-westerly corner of the fifteenth ward, at a point in the middle of Fourteenth street . . .

THE BROOKLYN BRIDGE - 1883

On May 24, 1883, the Brooklyn Bridge across the East River was officially opened to the public. The bridge was truly one of the marvels of the time. The following selection describes the opening ceremonies of this important event.

(Source: New York Times, May 25, 1883.)

The Brooklyn bridge was successfully opened yesterday. A fairer day for the ceremony could not have been chosen. The sky was cloudless, and the heat from the brightly shining sun was tempered by a cool breeze. The pleasant weather brought visitors by the thousands from all around. Special trains were run from Philadelphia and Easton, Penn. and from Long Island points. Extra cars were attached to regular trains, and then there was barely standing room. It is estimated that over 50,000 people came in by the railroads alone, and swarms by the Sound boats and by the ferryboats helped to swell the crowds in both cities.

The opening of the bridge was decidedly Brooklyn's celebration. New York's participation in it was meagre, save as to the crowd which thronged her streets. Some of the Exchanges and business houses down town were closed; others stopped business about noon, but as a rule the stores were open as usual, and as a rule, too, patrons were as numerous as on the other days of the year, when no Brooklyn bridges are opened. The crowd from outside, with curious New-Yorkers, combined to give to the vicinity of Madison-square, to Broadway, and to City Hall Park, the customary gala-day crowds. Thousands of people crowded each one of the places named. The windows, the balconies, and the roofs of Broadway buildings had their throngs. There was no general decoration beyond the display of the American flags. These were flown wherever there was a staff surmounting a building, and in themselves gave the City a holiday appearance. Aside from this display there were not more than a score of buildings that were decorated. Of these the most noticeable were in the vicinity of the New-York approach at the publication offices of the Sun and the Staats-Zeitung. Festoons of bunting graced a half-dozen Broadway fronts. While the crowd of strangers were gathering along the line of march Superintendent Walling was personally superintending the police arrangements up town and Inspector Murray doing a like service with the large force detailed from the various precincts down town. The arrangements were well executed, and as a result there was no delay caused by the blocking of the streets. At about 9 o'clock a gang of workmen removed the unsightly fence which has been in front of the New-York approach and an equally impassable fence of about 50 policemen took its place.

Promptly at 11:15 A.M. the assembly was sounded at the armory of the Seventh Regiment, the escort to the President, the Governor, the Mayor and the other more or less distinguished guests. A half-hour later the regiment had been equalized aby Adjt. Rand into 14 platoons of 20 files, or 40 men, each. A guard was detailed, and at 11:45, the regiment, Col. Clark commanding, left its armory and, headed by Cappa's band of 70 pieces and a drum corps of 22, started on its march. The men were dressed in Summer uniform, gray coats, white trousers, and white helmets. From Sixty-seventh-street and Fourth-avenue, through Sixty-sixth street and down Madison avenue, the regiment moved to Fifty-seventh street. Passing through that street to Fifth avenue, the regiment marched down the avenue with the perfect front and the long, swinging steps which have always marked it, to Fifth-Avenue Hotel. At Twenty-third-street and Fifth-avenue the regiment halted. Two companies marched into Twenty-third-street, presented arms, and received the guests of the day. These occupied 24 carriages. In the first of these were seated President Arthur and Mayor Edson. . . .

Never in the history of Brooklyn did that city of anniversary events wear such a garment of colors as she did yesterday. To Brooklyn, which conceived the idea of a bridge and which furnished the bulk of the enormous sum required to build it, must be rewarded the lead in the celebration. The city fathers set the example and the citizens vied with one another in following it. There are 500 miles of streets in the city. It would be no exaggeration to say that from every block of that vast distance fluttered a flag or floated a lantern. It was in the lower end of the city, in the vicinity of the City Hall and on Columbia Heights in particular, that the decorative display was so attractive and in some instances so novel in its character. At an early hour in the morning a man crawled up the sides of the City Hall cupola and seated himself astride the neck of the blindfolded figure of Justice. He was joined by others, and when they had concluded their labors a pair of glistening bronze scales swung in their accustomed position, the flagstaff had been righted, and the national colors were flying from its truck. Far below it, from the staff on the roof, fluttered in the breeze the colors of the city itself, displaying the old Dutch motto "Een draght macht mocht." Every window in the building had its shield with its draping of miniature flags. The Ionic columns of the portico were draped with bunting. A similar display of flags and shields was made at the windows of the Municipal Building in the rear of the City Hall, and the dome of the Courthouse adjoining was gorgeous in its dress of flying colors. The buildings about the City Hall square were heavy with bunting. Fulton-street in both directions, Court street, Joralemon street, Remsen and Montague streets, and Washington street and Myrtle-avenue, all entering the square from as many different directions, presented a magnificent view of flags of all nations and Chinese lanterns strung from basement to roof on the private dwellings. The storekeepers on both sides of Fulton-street, from City Hall to ferry, gave up their windows and doorways to decorations. A jeweler had removed his wares and in the corner window had outlined a miniature representation of the bridge, massive gold chains forming the cables. In the window of another store was a floral piece, an excellent imitation of the bridge, 8 feet in length. Over the main entrance to the store was a large banner on which were inscribed the words: "Roebling -- One of the few immortal names that were not born to die." On a transparency was inscribed the quotation: "Babylon had her hanging gardens, Egypt her Pyramids, Athens her Acropolis, Rome her Coliseum -- so Brookly has her bridge. Over its broad roadway the teeming millions of the two cities may pass; under its spacious arch the commerce of the world may pass." Some windows were occupied with portraits or busts of the late Henry C. Murphy, John A. Roebling, and the present chief engineer of the bridge, Col. Washington A. Roebling. . . .

All the time that the services were going on crowds of people were passing and repassing over the bridge. The policemen guarding either end were constantly on the alert, scanning the tickets of those who entered, turning deaf ears to the many appeals of the ticketless, and occasionally closing an eye while some favored friend passed in. In the crowds hanging about the entrances enterprising speculators were selling tickets for which they obrained from 75 cents to $3 50, according to the apparent ability of the purchaser. Upon the bridge the military were doing picket duty, the Seventh Regiment upon the carriage-way of the down-town side and the New York half of the passenger walk and the Twenty-third of Brooklyn, upon the remainder. Policemen of both cities were walking here and there, but whether on duty or for pleasure was not apparent. For fully three hours the stream of pedestrians was uninterrupted, the two carriageways and the footwalk being used indiscriminately. Most of them were evidently City people, and among them were many ladies and some children. With the ending of the ceremonies, the military were withdrawn. After 5 o'clock admission to the bridge was refused even to ticket-holders. Speculators continued to sell tickets, however. The police began clearing the bridge at 5?30, and it took until nearly 7 o'clock to finish the work. The crowd pressed in upon the lines of police drawn across the entrance on Chatham street, and were roughly handled in some instances. Still, no unnecessary violence seemed to be used. A man who claimed to be a Deputy Sheriff from Brooklyn broke through the lines, and in an altercation with Sergt. Kale of the Fourteenth Precinct, over his detention struck the Sergeant fair in the face. He was arrested. The crowd was good-natured, and save for a desire to get up to and on the bridge made little trouble.

Among the many parties made up to attend the opening ceremonies was what Mrs. Roebling called her "bridge party," and was composed of a few friends from Trenton, New York, and Brooklyn. . . .

If yesterday's traffic across the Brooklyn bridge demonstrated anything, it was that the volume of travel, particularly from the New York end, was regulated and altogether limited by the facilities for getting upon the bridge. Whether this will prove the case after the curious have satisfied their desires and have seen all that there is to be seen by a personal inspection of the structure from end to end is a matter of speculation with the bridge Trustees. The terminal facilities so far as New York is concerned were out of proportion altogether with the demand made upon them yesterday. It could hardly have been otherwise, with a station of the elevated railroad directly in front of the New York approach, with a string of horse cars passing every moment of the day, and with a want of suitable outlets to the opposite side of Manhattan Island. There was a crush of foot passengers from 11 o'clock in the morning until 7 o'clock at night. They collected at the entrance, compressed themselves into a funnel about 15 feet in width, and then ran the gantlet, one by one, of the toll-takers. Once past these officers, the footpath for a brief space widened out, and in this the crowd shook itself and took breath for the long journey across the wonderful bridge. Once outside the brick and iron building there was no crowding and no difficulty in making an easy trip on foot to the Brooklyn side. It was a strong tide, however, as he found out who stopped for a moment to lean over the railing and gaze at the panorama spread out over miles of space. He was jostled in the most uncomfortable manner. This tide swept along, keeping to the right and occupying just about half of the 15 feet into which the promenade had once more compressed itself. An equally strong tide of human beings occupied the other half setting in from Brooklyn toward New York. There was no clashing between them. For eight hours this condition of affairs existed on the bridge. Two bicycle rides, one of this City and one of St. Louis, threaded their way among the crowd, and claim the honor of being the first wheelmen to cross the bridge. Pick-pockets were buy, especially toward night. Two watches were found in the pocket of a colored thief. A Brooklyn man lost a valuable watch, but caught the culprit and recovered the timepiece. Another Brooklyn man was not so fortunate. There was more strength developed in the flow Brooklynward as the evening approached and the Brooklyn workmen and workwomen began their journey to their homes. A limited number of policemen was stationed at the New York entrance during the day. They were mor ornamental than useful, and were not particularly to be commended for either characteristic. Had there been enough of them, and had their activity been even at par, they might have prevented a great deal of the trouble and annoyance to which the foot passengers and the drivers of vehicles were subjected. Horse cars, wagons, and carriages became helplessly entangled, and were no sooner straightened out than they again became hopelessly confused. Whenever friction occurred foot passengers were inconvenienced in consequence. The difficulty of getting into line and preparing to enter the funnel was quite enough without having that of inconvenience by horse car and wagon added to it. At 6 o'clock Printinghous-square presented a remarkable spectacle. A mass of men, women, and boys almost completely covered it, awaiting their turn to pass over to Brooklyn. Wedged in among this throng were horse cars and vehicles of every description. . . .

CLEANING THE CITY'S STREETS - 1897

The problem of cleaning the city's streets has always been, and continues to be of major concern. The following excerpt is part of a report submitted by George F. Waring Jr., Commissioner of Street Cleaning, describing the factors in the cost of street cleaning, and the problem of snow removal.

(Source: <u>Report of the Department of Street Cleaning of the City of New York for 1895, 1896, 1897,</u> New York, 1897.)

COLONEL GEORGE E. WARING, JR.,
    Commissioner of Street Cleaning:

SIR -- I have the honor to submit herewith a report upon the principal factors which make up the cost of street cleaning in the City of New York, their distribution throughout the city and the percentage effect of each upon the total cost.

The term "street cleaning," as here used, applies only to the work of the sweepers and has no reference to the cost of horses, drivers or carts to remove the sweepings, nor to any other of the expenses of the Department.

Last autumn a series of sweeping tests was made to determine the areas of asphalt, granite and Belgian pavements, respectively, which could be kept clean by one man, and the foremen were instructed to report in each case the condition of the pavement and the amount of traffic. But it was found that the differences on each class of pavement were not all to be accounted for by the dissimilarity in condition and in amount of traffic, and the present report has grown out of the desire to learn all the causes of variation.

The information has been gained through a block-by-block measurement of the area of paved streets cleaned by the Department -- the measurements having been made during the winter by the section foremen, under the supervision of the District Superintendents; a statement for each block of (1) its kind of pavement -- asphalt, granite, Belgian or other; (2) the condition of the pavement -- good, fair or bad; (3) the amount of traffic -- light, medium or heavy; (4) the amount of car track, if any -- single, double, triple or quadruple; (5) the kind of rail -- flat, grooved, T or steam T; (6) the amount of sanding of the track -- little or much; (7) the amount of street sprinkling -- whether it is sprinkling or flooding the street with so much water as to make slush; (8) the presence or absence of elevated railroad pillars and overhead structure; (9) the character of the population; (10) the number of schools; (11) the presence of market-stores, or (12) push-carts; (13) the vicinity of unpaved streets.

There are other conditions which affect the cost of cleaning, but nearly all of them are either temporary -- such as building operations, or under the control of the District Superintendent -- such as the energy and judgment of the sweeper, or under the general control of the Department -- such as the quality of brooms, etc. The thirteen items above mentioned were considered to be beyond the control of the Department, and, with the exception of the schools and street sprinkling, beyond its influence.

Having selected these factors, in consultation with the superintendents, as having the most important bearing upon the subject in hand, and the measurements above mentioned having been made, there was prepared a tabulated statement for each district, which statements form the series of tables No. 1 of this report. It is to be noted concerning these tables that the figures in some columns, such as condition of pavement, amount of traffic and character of population, are statements of opinion rather than results of measurement, and that some allowance must be made for the "personal equation," since what is considered good condition of pavement or good character of population by one man might by another be considered, in either case, only fair. It is believed, however, that with few exceptions the statements may be taken as having nearly the same relative value. . . .

COLONEL GEORGE E. WARING, JR.,
    Commissioner of Street Cleaning:

SIR -- The following historical sketch and report relates to the work done in snow and ice removal under the various Commissioners from the year 1881, when the Department of Street Cleaning was taken from the control of the Police Department and became a separate branch of the city government, to the 15th of January, 1895, comparing the results achieved with those since that date under the present administration. The data for the comparison have been very carefully and exhaustively compiled from the various reports in the "City Record," and checked with the voucher books and records in the Department archives. In the few instances of difference between the sources of information the latter authority has been uniformly chosen.

NECESSITY FOR REMOVAL.

The question of snow removal has always been one of the most vexatious problems confronting the various administrations. The removal of "new fallen snow from leading thoroughfares and such other streets and avenues as may be found practicable" is a duty made obligatory upon the Commissioner by law, and, with each year, the moral obligation to the vast traffic interests of congested Manhattan Island becomes more insistent. Of late also the question of the health of the community has entered with great force into any consideration of the subject. . . .

THE GREATER NEW YORK CHARTER - 1898

The Greater New York Charter, which united the
five boroughs went into effect on January 1, 1898.
It had become law on May 4, 1897, and gave the
greater city an area of 359 square miles, and a
population of more than 3,100,000. The preface
to this very important charter follows.

(Source: The Greater New York Charter, Mark Ash, ed., Albany, 1897.)

The movement for consolidation of the cities of New York, Brooklyn and contiguous territory, which had its inception in 1890, and culminated seven years later in the Charter appearing herein, will mark an epoch in the history of municipalities in this western continent. Beginning with the preliminary stage of investigation by a legislative Commission of Municipal Consolidation Inquiry, the great project advanced, step by step, despite all obstacles, until, in 1896, the union became an accomplished fact, and a commission was appointed to prepare the organic law of the new city.

The commission, noted for the distinguished character of its members, fitted by experience and calling for the important civic duty confided to them, appointed, in the first instance, a sub-committee on draft, which presented to the main body, as the result of its labors, a proposed charter, with an exhaustive report, discussing the features thereof. This draft was then taken up by the entire commission, and after discussion at public hearings, and in executive session, resulting in changes and amendments, the Charter and supplementary legislation, almost as finally enacted, were presented to the legislature by the commission, on February 18, 1897, with its report. These two exhaustive reports of the commission and the sub-committee on draft, affording the best commentary upon the Charter, have been reprinted in full, with all the legislation touching the consolidation, in the Introductory.

The conspicuous features of the Greater New York Charter are the borough system, with its twenty-two boards, vested with power to initiate local improvements; the municipal assembly, consisting of two chambers; and the single-headed independent departments, constituting the board of public improvements. Aside from these important provisions, and some minor departures, the scheme of the Charter follows in the main the lines of the New York City Consolidation Act, passed in 1882. The plan, therefore, pursued in the present work is that adopted by the author in his edition of the Consolidation Act, published in 1891, which received the approval of the profession.

The commission which prepared the Charter, neither in its report to the legislature accompanying the same, nor in the report of its sub-committee on draft, indicated the statutory sources of its various provisions. The different sections have been carefully examined and compared, and the derivatory statutes noted, wherever possible. To avoid confusion, in cases in which the provisions of the Charter were simply re-enactments of the Consolidation Act, the sections of the latter have been given, without referring to prior statutes revised in the Consolidation Act. However, for the convenience of those desiring to trace these sections to their earlier sources, the author has reprinted from his edition of the Consolidation Act the table showing what acts were included in the same.

The annotations of judicial decisions under the various sections have not been confined merely to authorities construing former statutes revised in the Charter, but the same include cases upon analogous provisions found in the charters of other municipalities in this State. All the authorities to and including the 151 N.Y., 15 Appellate Division, I) Miscellaneous and 44 N.Y. Supp., have been examined and cited.

The Charter, unlike the Consolidation Act, is not complete in itself. It extends many of the provisions of the Consolidation Act and other statutes of a general and permanent character to the new city, either specifically or by general language. The limitations of this work forbid the reprinting of all the statutes thus continued in force by the Charter. . . .

By section 1585 of the Charter, the public administrator is made a county officer, and the present statutes governing his powers and duties are declared to remain unaffected. These regulations are set out at length, with annotations of cases, in Appendix XI.

The sections of the Consolidation Act governing liens upon municipal contracts, which remain in force by section 1610 of the Charter, are placed in Appendix X.

The basis of representation in the board of aldermen, and the council, constituting the municipal assembly, being the assembly districts included within the Greater New York, the apportionment of these assembly districts made in 1895, pursuant to constitutional requirement, has been reprinted in Appendix III.

In view of the many provisions of the State Constitution concerning the government of cities, limitation of their indebtedness, and restrictions upon local legislation, city officials, civil service, and the like, the author has collated all the pertinent sections covering the subject in Appendix II. In connection with this branch of the work, especial care has been taken to give full notes of the cases interpreting these constitutional limitations.

For the purpose of local improvements and the creation of governing boards thereof, the territory of the city has been divided by the Charter into twenty-two districts, co-extensive with the senatorial districts provided by the Constitution, which districts will also be found in Appendix II.

The Royal English Colonial Charters have been reprinted in Appendix XII, for reference as to the continued vested rights of the city.

As before stated, the Consolidation Act, and all acts of the legislature affecting the local government of the City of New York not inconsistent with the Charter or revised therein, being continued in force, the author has prepared a table of all the sections of the Consolidation Act, showing which have been revised in the Charter, which repealed or superseded, and those still in force or unaffected, with references to the section reprinted in the appendixes. In addition, the statutes relating to the City of New York passed by the legislature from January 1, 1882 (when the Consolidation Act was deemed enacted), to and including the session of 1897, and which are not repealed or temporary, have been collated by their titles and subject-matter in a table, divided, for convenience of reference, under the same chapter and title headings as those of the Charter.

THE TENEMENT HOUSE PROBLEM - 1900

In 1900, the New York State Legislature created
the New York State Tenement Commission.
Lawrence Veiller and Robert W. de Forest were
its leaders. The following is a small portion
of a report submitted by the Commission.

(Source: <u>Report of the New York State Tenement House Commission of 1900,</u> New York, 1900.)

. . .Some knowledge of the prevailing kind of New York tenement house must necessarily precede any consideration of its evils and their remedies. It is known as the "double-decker," "dumb-bell" tenement, a type which New York has the unenviable distinction of having invented. It is a type unknown to any other city in America or Europe.

Although the housing problem is one of the leading political questions of the day in England, the conditions which exist there are ideal compared to the conditions in New York. The tall tenement house, accommodating as many as 100 to 150 persons in one building, extending up six or seven stories into the air, with dark, unventilated rooms, is unknown in London or in any other city of Great Britain. It was first constructed in New York about the year 1879, and with slight modifications has been practically the sole type of building erected since, and is the type of the present day. It is a building usually five or six or even seven stories high, about 25 feet wide, and built upon a lot of land of the same width and about 100 feet deep. The building as a rule extends back 90 feet, leaving the small space of ten feet unoccupied at the rear, so that the back rooms may obtain some light and air. This space has continued to be left open only because the law has compelled it. Upon the entrance floor there are generally two stores, one on each side of the guilding, and these sometimes have two or three living rooms back of them. In the centre is the entrance hallway, a long corridor less than 3 feet wide and extending back 60 feet in length. This hallway is nearly always totally dark, receiving no light except that from the street door and a faint light that comes from the small windows opening upon the stairs, which are placed at one side of the hallway. Each floor above is generally divided into four sets of apartments, there being seven rooms on each side of the hall, extending back from the street to the rear of the building. The front apartments generally consist of four rooms each and the rear apartments of three rooms, making altogether fourteen upon each floor, or in a seven-story house eighty-four rooms exclusive of the stores and rooms back of them. Of these fourteen rooms on each floor, only four receive direct light and air from the street or from the small yard at the back of the building. Generally, along each side of the building is what is termed an "air shaft," being an indentation of the wall to a depth of about 28 inches, and extending in length for a space of from 50 to 60 feet. This shaft is entirely enclosed on four sides, and is, of course, the full height of the building, often from 60 to 72 feet high. The ostensible purpose of the shaft is to provide light and air to the five rooms on each side of the house which get no direct light and air from the street or yard; but as the shafts are narrow and high, being enclosed on all four sides, and without any intake of air at the bottom, these rooms obtain, instead of fresh air and sunshine, foul air and semi-darkness. Indeed it is questionable whether the rooms would not be more habitable and more sanitary with no shaft at all, depending for their light and air solely upon the front and back rooms into which they open; for each family, besides having the foul air from its own rooms to breathe, is compelled to breathe the emanations from the rooms of some eleven other families; nor is this all, these shafts act as conveyors of noise, odors, and disease, and when fire breaks out serve as inflammable flues, often rendering it impossible to save the buildings from destruction.

A family living in such a building pays for four rooms of this kind a rent of from $12 to $18 a month. Of these four rooms only two are large enough to be deserving of the name of rooms. The front one is generally about 10 feet 6 inches wide by 11 feet 3 inches long; this the family use as a parlor, and often at night, when the small bedrooms opening upon the air shaft are so close and ill-ventilated that sleep is impossible, mattresses are dragged upon the floor of the parlor, and there the family sleep, all together in one room. In summer the small bedrooms are so hot and stifling that a large part of the tenement house population sleep on the roofs, the sidewalks, and the fire-escapes. The other room, the kitchen, is generally the same size as the parlor upon which it opens, and receives all its light and air from the "air shaft," or such a supply as may come to it from the front room. Behind these two rooms are the bedrooms, so called, whic which are hardly more than closets, being each about 7 feet wide and 8 feet 6 inches long, hardly large enough to contain a bed. These rooms get no light and air whatsoever, except that which comes from the "air shaft," and except on the highest stories are generally almost totally dark. Upon the opposite side of the public hall is an apartment containing four exactly similar rooms, and at the rear of the building there are, instead of four rooms on each side of the hallway, but three, one of the bedrooms being dispensed with. For these three rooms in the rear the rent is generally throughout the city from $10 to $15 a month. In the public hallway, opposite the stairs, there are provided two water-closets, each water-closet being used in common by two families and being lighted and ventilated by the "air shaft," which also lights and ventilates all the bedrooms. In the newer building thre is frequently provided, in the hallway between the two closets, a dumb-waiter for the use of the tenants.

It is not to be wondered at, therefore, that with such a kind of tenement house repeated all over the different parts of this city, and forming practically the only kind of habitation for the great mass of the people, the tenement house system has become fraught with so much danger to the welfare of the community. . . .

A POEM FOR NEW YORK - 1910

    Many writers have used New York City as a subject. Even the great Walt Whitman was moved by the contrasts of the city to write this poem.

(Source: Walt Whitman, <u>Leaves of Grass</u>, New York and London, 1910.)

I was asking for something specific and perfect for my city,
Whereupon lo! upsprang the aboriginal name.

Now I see what there is in a name, a word, liquid, sane, unruly, musical, self-sufficient,
I see that the word of my city is that word from of old,
Because I see that word nested in nests of water-bays, superb,
Rich, hemm'd thick all around with sailships and steamships, an island sixteen miles long, solid-founded,
Numberless crowded streets, high growths of iron, slender, strong, light, splendidly uprising toward clear skies,
Tides swift and ample, well-lived by me, toward sundown,
The flowing sea-currents, the little islands, larger adjoining islands, the heights, the villas,
The countless masts, the white shore-steamers, the lighters, the ferry-boats, the black sea-steamers well-model'd,
The down-town streets, the jobbers' houses of business, the houses of business of the ship-merchants and money-brokers, the river-streets,
Immigrants arriving, fifteen or twenty thousand in a week,
The carts hauling goods, the manly race of drivers of horses, the brown-faced sailors.

The summer air, the bright sun shining, and the sailing clouds aloft,
The winter snows, the sleigh-bells, the broken ice in the river, passing along up or down with the flood-tide or ebb-tide,
The mechanics of the city, the masters, well-form'd, beautiful-faced, looking you straight in the eyes,
Trottoirs throng'd, vehicles, Broadway, the women, the shops and shows,
A million people--manners free and superb--open voices--hospitality--the most courageous and friendly young men,
City of hurried and sparkling waters! city of spires and masts!
City nested in bays! my city!

THE PORT AUTHORITY OF NEW YORK - 1921

On April 2, 1921, the States of New York and New Jersey entered into a novel agreement, which created the Port of New York Authority. A portion of the State Legislature's act establishing this new authority follows.

(Source: Laws of New York, Albany, 1921.)

In the year eighteen hundred and thirty-four the states of New York and New Jersey did enter into an agreement determining the rights and obligations of the two states in and around the waters between the two states, especially in and around the bay of New York and the Hudson river; and. . . .

Since that time the commerce of the port of New York has greatly developed and increased and the territory in and around the port has become commercially one center or district. . . .

It is confidently believed that a better co-ordination of terminal, transportation and other facilities of commerce in and through the port of New York, will result in great prosperity, benefiting the nation, as well as the states of New York and New Jersey; and. . .

The future development of such terminal, transportation and other facilities of commerce will require the expenditure of large sums of money and the cordial co-operation of the states of New York and New Jersey in the encouragement of the expenditure of capital, and in the formulation and execution of various physical plans; and

Such result can best be accomplished through the cooperation of the two states by and through a joint or common Port Authority. . . .

The said states of New Jersey and New York agree to and amend the existing agreement of eighteen hundred and thirty-four in the following respects:

ARTICLE I.

They agree to and pledge, each to the other, faithful co-operation in the planning and development of the port of New York, holding in high trust for the benefit of the nation and the blessings and natural advantages thereof.

ARTICLE II.

To that end the two states do agree that there shall be and they do hereby create a district to be known as the "Port of New York District" (for brevity hereinafter referred to as "The District") which shall embrace the territory being described as follows. . . .

THE CHARTER OF 1936

The following is an excerpt from the new city charter adopted by the voters on November 3, 1936. Its most innovative change from past charters, was the provision for the abolition of the Board of Aldermen, and the creation of a small City Council to be chosen by proportional representation.

(Source: <u>Report of the New York City Charter Revision Commission</u>, August 17, 1936; <u>Charter For the City of New York</u>, November 3, 1936.)

ELECTION OF COUNCILMEN BY PROPORTIONAL REPRESENTATION.

Application of Chapter.

1001. This chapter shall take effect and be a part of the charter if, and only if, the system of proportional representation herein provided for the election of the council is approved by the electors of the city when the question is submitted to them. If such system is so approved, subdivision b of section twenty-two shall be of no effect.

Effect of adoption.

1002. a. Councilmen shall be elected by the system of proportional representation provided for in this chapter, from each borough in proportion to the number of valid votes cast for councilmen in the borough as hereinafter provided.

b. Elections of councilmen by proportional representation shall be conducted by the election authorities prescribed by the election law, and the provisions of the election law with respect to nomination of candidates, declination of nominations, filling vacancies, notices to candidates, objections to petitions, rulings thereon, judicial proceedings and all other matters so far as applicable shall govern except in the method of counting the votes for councilmen and except as provision is otherwise made herein.

c. The local legislative body of the city shall have power to make administrative regulations, not inconsistent with the provisions of this charter, which they consider needful or desirable for the conduct of elections of councilmen by proportional representation and for the prevention of fraud in such elections. The board of elections shall have power to make such regulations not inconsistent with such administrative regulations.

Districts.

1003. Each borough shall be a single separate district for the election of councilmen by proportional representation and shall elect one councilmen within it. A remainder of fifty thousand such voters or more shall entitle a borough to one additional councilman, and each borough shall be entitled to at least one councilman.

Nominations.

1004. a. NOMINATION BY PETITION. In the nomination of candidates for councilman no primaries shall be held. All nominations shall be by nominating petitions in accordance with the provisions of the election law for independent nominations so for as applicable except as herein otherwise provided.

b. NUMBER OF SIGNATURES. A nominating petition for the office of councilman for any borough shall be signed by not fewer than two thousand electors who have registered as voters of such borough within eighteen months previous to the filing of the petition.

c. SEPARATE PETITIONS AND SIGNERS REQUIRED. Each candidate shall be nominated by a separate petition and no elector shall sign more than one such petition. Should an elector sign more than one such petition, his signature shall be void except upon the original or supplementary petition signed by him which is first validly filed.

d. PARTY NAMES. Nominating petitions may specify party, group or individual designations for the candidates. They shall contain no emblems.

e. PARTY AFFILIATION OF SIGNERS DISREGARDED. Any elector otherwise qualified may sign any petition regardless of his party affiliation and regardless of whether he has voted in a party primary.

f. TIME OF SIGNING. A signature made earlier than one hundred days before the election shall not be counted.

g. TIME OF FILING PETITIONS. Petitions may be filed at any time before the last date for the filing of independent nominating petitions.

Ballots and voting.

1005. Unless voting machines are provided as permitted under the terms of section one thousand eight, councilmen shall be voted for, in accordance with the instructions provided in this section, on paper ballots separate and distinct from ballots used for any other office or question, and the ballot boxes used for the election of councilmen shall be separate and distinct from ballot boxes used for any other office or question. Each voter shall be given one ballot for councilmen from the borough in which he resides. The ballots shall conform to the provisions of the election law for paper ballots for general officers, so far as applicable, with the following exceptions:

1. ROTATION OF NAMES. The names of the candidates shall be printed in the alphabetical order of their surnames, except that they shall be rotated by election districts as provided in this subdivision, so that each name shall appear first and in each other position in an equal number, as nearly as possible, of the election districts of the borough. In such rotation all the districts in the borough shall be treated as a single continuous series, beginning with the first election district of the first assembly district and continuing with the second and subsequent election districts of the first assembly district in numerical order, then with all the election districts of the second assembly district in numerical order, and so on to the last election district of the last assembly district. In the first election district in this series the names of the candidates shall appear in alphabetical order. In the second they shall appear in the same order except that the first name shall appear

last. In each district the names shall appear in the same order as in the same order as in the preceding district, except that the first name in that preceding district shall appear last.

2. PARTY DESIGNATIONS. The ballots shall contain no emblems and only one square for voting before each condidate's name. After each candidate's name shall be printed the party, group or individual designations specified on his nominating peitions, except as in this paragraph otherwise provided. If there are two or more such designations to follow a candidate's name, they shall appear in alphabetical order, except that the names of political parties shall precede other designations. Each county committee of a political party or the authorized officers of an independent body shall have the right to certify to the board of elections, not later than twenty days before the election, which of the candidates using the name of the party in the committee's borough or the name of the independent body shall be considered official candidates of the party or of the independent body, and the name of that party or of the independent body shall not accompany the names of any other candidates on the ballot. . . .

THE CHARTER OF 1961

In 1961, the voters of New York City approved the adoption of a new city charter, which changed a number of the structural and administrative procedures of the Charter of 1936. A small part of this new charter follows.

(Source: <u>New York City Charter</u>, John B. Martin, ed., New York, November 7, 1961.)

INTRODUCTORY
The City
    1. The City of New York as now existing shall continue with the boundaries and with the powers, rights and property, and subject to the obligations and liabilities which exist at the time when this charter shall take effect.
The Boroughs
    2. The boroughs of the city are continued as existing at the time of the adoption of this charter.

CHAPTER 1
MAYOR
Office; Powers
    3. The mayor shall be the chief executive officer of the city. He may, by executive order, at any time, create or abolish bureaus, division or positions within his executive office as he may deem necessary to fulfill his duties. He may from time to time by executive order, delegate to or withdraw from any member of said office, specified functions, powers and duties, except his power to act on local laws or resolutions of the council, to act as a magistrate or to appoint or remove officials. Every such order shall be filed with the city clerk.

Election; Term; Salary
    4. The mayor shall be elected at the general election in the year nineteen hundred sixty-five and every four years thereafter. He shall hold office for a term of four years commencing on the first day of January after his election. The salary of the mayor shall be fifty thousand dollars a year. (As amended by Local Law 96 of 1961.)

Annual Statement to Council
    5. The mayor shall communicate to the council at least once in each year a statement of the finances, government and affairs of the city with a summary statement of the activities of the agencies of the city.

Heads of Departments; Appoint; Remove
    6. a. The mayor shall appoint the heads of departments, all

commissioners and all other officers not elected by the people, except as otherwise provided by law.

b. The mayor, whenever in his judgment the public interest shall so require, may remove from office any public officer holding office by appointment from a mayor of the city, except officers for whose removal other provision is made by law. No public officer shall hold his office for any specific term, except as otherwise provided by law.

Deputy Mayors; Executive Office of Mayor

7. The mayor shall have power to appoint two or more deputy mayors. Except as otherwise directed by the mayor, one deputy shall act as the representative of the mayor on boards and committees, exercise jurisdiction over all legislative and ceremonial functions, by policy advisor to the mayor, supervise the executive office and perform such other duties as the mayor may assign to him, and one deputy shall supervise the other offices and departments of the city, except the law department, the department of investigation and such other agencies or bureaus as the mayor, from time to time may direct.

General Powers

8. a. The mayor, subject to this charter, shall exercise all the powers vested in the city, except as otherwise provided by law.

b. The mayor shall be a magistrate.

c. Notwithstanding any other provision of law, the mayor shall have the powers of a finance board under the local finance law and may exercise such powers without regard to any provision of law prescribing the voting strength required for a resolution or action of such finance board, provided, however, that whenever the mayor determines that obligations should be issued and the amount thereof, he shall certify such determination to the comptroller who shall thereupon determine the nature and term of such obligations and shall arrange for the issuance thereof. (As added by Chapter 998 of the Laws of 1962).

Removal of Mayor

9. The mayor may be removed from office by the governor upon charges and after service upon him of a copy of the charges and an opportunity to be heard in his defense. Pending the preparation and disposition of charges, the governor may suspend the mayor for a period not exceeding thirty days.

Succession

10. a. In case of the suspension of the mayor from office, his temporary inability to discharge the powers and duties of his office by reason of sickness or otherwise, or his absence from the city, the powers and duties of the office of mayor shall devolve upon the president of the council or the comptroller in that order of succession until the suspension, inability or absence shall cease. While so acting temporarily as mayor neither the president of the council nor the comptroller shall exercise any power of appointment to or removal from office or any power lawfully delegated by the mayor to a deputy mayor whether before

or after the commencement of such suspension, inability or absence; and shall not, until such suspension, inability or absence shall have continued nine days, sign, approve or disapprove any local law or resolution, unless the period during which the mayor can act thereon would expire during said nine days in which case the president of the council or the comptroller shall have the power to disapprove the same within forty-eight hours before the time to act expires.

b. In the case of a failure of a person elected as mayor to qualify, or a vacancy in the office caused by the mayor's resignation, removal, death or permanent inability to discharge his powers and duties, such powers and duties shall devolve upon the president of the council, the comptroller or a person selected pursuant to subdivision b of section twenty-seven, in that order of succession, until a new mayor shall be elected as provided herein. If the vacancy shall occur before the twentieth day of September in any year, such vacancy shall be filled in the general election held in that year, otherwise it shall be filled in the general election held in the following year. The term of the person then elected mayor shall begin on January first after such election and shall expire on the date when the term of the mayor originally elected would have expired. Upon the commencement of the term of the thus elected mayor, the president of the council or the comptroller then acting as mayor shall complete the term of the office to which he was elected if any remains.

CHAPTER 2
COUNCIL

Legislative Power

21. In addition to the other powers vested in it by this charter, the council shall be vested with the legislative power of the city, and shall be the local legislative body of the city.

Composition of Council

22. a. The council shall consist of the president of the council and of other members termed councilmen.

b. One councilman shall be elected from each senate district as now or hereafter constituted lying wholly or partly within the city, and two councilmen shall be elected at large from each of the boroughs.

c. No party or independent body as defined in the election law shall nominate more than one candidate for councilman to be elected at large in any borough.

d. Each elector shall have the right to vote for not more than one candidate at large and the two candidates receiving the largest number of votes in each borough shall be elected.

e. The first election of councilmen at large shall be held at the general election in the year nineteen hundred sixty-three and the terms of councilmen so elected shall expire coterminously with those of the councilmen then in office. . . .

THE CITY UNIVERSITY - 1961

On April 11, 1961, the State Legislature created the City University of New York, by combining the various public owned and operated colleges in the New York City area. The following selection describes the creation of this great urban university.

(Source: Laws of New York, 1961.)

The People of the State of New York, represented in Senate and Assembly, do enact as follows:

Section 1. The education law is hereby amended by adding thereto a new section, to be section two hundred thirty-seven thereof, to read as follows:

237. Regents plan for higher education including approved plans of state university and city university of New York

1. The regents shall, once every four years, review the proposed plan and recommendations required to be submitted by the state university trustees pursuant to section three hundred fifty-four of this chapter and the proposed plan and recommendations of the board of higher education in the city of New York required to be submitted pursuant to section sixty-two hundred two of this chapter, and upon approval of such plans by the regents they shall be incorporated into a regents plan or general revision thereof for the expansion and development of higher education in the state. Such regents plan shall include the plan and recommendations proposed by the state university trustees and the plan and recommendations proposed by the board of higher education in the city of New York and may include plans with respect to other matters not comprehended within the plan of the state and city universities, including but not limited to improving institutional management and resources, instruction and guidance programs, financial assistance to students and extension of educational opportunities through library resources and television. In the development of such plans due recognition shall be given to that historical development of higher education in the state which has been accomplished through the establishment and encouragement of private institutions. In determining the need for additional educational facilities in a particular area, the plans and facilities of existing public and private institutions shall be fully evaluated and considered.

2. During the calendar year nineteen hundred sixty-four and each fourth year thereafter the regents shall evaluate all available information with respect to the plans and facilities of private institutions and shall review and act upon the proposed plan and recommendations of the state university trustees and upon the proposed plan and recommendations of the board of higher education in the city of New York and incorporate such information, recommendations and each of the component plans so acted upon into a tentative regents plan or general revi-

sion thereof for the expansion and development of higher education in the state. Copies of such tentative regents plan or general revision thereof, as the case may be, shall be made available to the trustees of the state university, the board of higher education in the city of New York and the governing boards of all other institutions of higher education admitted to the university of the state of New York. Thereafter, after giving due notice, the regents shall conduct one or more hearings on such tentative regents plan or general revision thereof.

3. The regents shall transmit their plan or general revision thereof for the expansion and development of higher education in the state to the governor and the legislature on or before the first day of December, nineteen hundred sixty-four and each fourth year thereafter, and such plan or general revision thereof shall become effective upon its approval by the governor.

4. Any modification recommended by the state university trustees or by the board of higher education in the city of New York to their respective plans, theretofore formulated and approved pursuant to section three hundred fifty-four or section sixty-two hundred two of this chapter shall be reviewed by the regents who may hold one or more hearings thereon after giving due notice thereof. As approved by the regents, such modification shall be made a part of the respective plans of the state university and of the city university and shall, together with any modifications the regents may make to that portion of their plan for the expansion and development of higher education in the state not comprehended in the plans of the state and city universities, be transmitted to the governor and the legislature, all of which shall then become effective upon approval by the governor as modifications of the regents plan. By the first day of November in each of the three years following the promulgation of the regents plan or general revision thereof, the regents shall summarize and report to the governor and the legislature any modifications made pursuant to this subdivision and shall include in such report a statement on the progress made in implementing the regents plan and their general recommendations with respect to higher education.

2. Subdivision one of section three hundred fifty-two of such law, as last amended by chapter seven hundred thirty-four of the laws of nineteen hundred fifty-one, is hereby amended to read as follows:

1. There is hereby created in the state education department and within the higher educational system of the state university of the state of New York as established under the board of regents a corporation to be known as the state university of New York which shall be responsible for the planning, supervision and administration of facilities and programs in accordance with the plan proposed by the state university trustees as approved by the regents pursuant to section two hundred thirty-seven of this chapter, and provisions for higher education supported in whole or in part with state moneys in accordance with the provisions of section three hundred fifty-eight hereof, and to perform such other duties as may be entrusted to it by law. Such corporation shall have the care, custody, control and management of the lands, grounds,

buildings, facilities and equipment used for the purposes of the state-operated institutions of the state university, and it shall have power to protect, preserve and improve the same.

3. Section three hundred fifty-four of such law, subdivision two having been amended by chapter two hundred ninety-nine of the laws of nineteen hundred fifty-five, and subdivision three having been amended by chapter six hundred ninety-eight of the laws of nineteen hundred forty-eight, is hereby repealed.

4. Such law is hereby amended by adding thereto a new section, to be section three hundred fifty-four, to read as follows:

354. Powers and duties of state university trustees planning functions

1. The state university trustees shall, once every four years, formulate a long-range state university plan or general revision thereof and make recommendations to the board of regents and the governor for the organization, development, coordination and expansion of the state university and for the establishment of community colleges in area suitable for and in need of such institutions, which plan and recommendations shall include the following:

    a. Plans for new curricula.
    b. Plans for new facilities.
    c. Plans for change in policies with respect to sudent admission.
    d. Potential student enrollments.
    e. Comments upon its relationship to other colleges and universities, public and private, within the state.

Prior to transmitting their long-range state university plan or general revision thereof to the board of regents and the governor the state university trustees may, after giving due notice, conduct one or more hearings on such plan.

2. During the calendar year nineteen hundred sixty-four and each fourth year thereafter the state university trustees shall transmit their proposed plan or general revision thereof to the board of regents and the governor on or before the twentieth day of September in each such year. Such plan shall be reviewed by the board of regents and shall be subject to approval by such board. As approved by the board of regents and incorporated into the regents plan or general revision thereof for the expansion and development of higher education in the state and, upon approval thereafter by the governor, such plan shall guide and determine the development and expansion of the state university and the establishment of community colleges until such plan is modified or revised in the manner provided herein.

3. By the twentieth day of September in each of the three years following the approval of the state university plan or general revision thereof pursuant to section two hundred thirty-seven of this chapter, the state university trustees shall report in writing to the board of regents and to the governor on the progress made in carrying out their responsibilities under such plan and their general recommendations with respect to public higher education, including recommendations as to modifications of such plan which the trustees deem essential to meet the then current demands upon public higher education. The state uni-

versity trustees may also at any other time propose modifications which they then deem essential or desirable with respect to such plan. They may, after giving due notice, conduct one or more hearings on such modifications and shall transmit their recommendations therefor to the board of regents and the governor. Such modifications shall be subject to approval by the regents and thereafter by the governor in the same manner as such plan or general revisions thereof.

5. The opening paragraph of subdivision one of section three hundred fifty-five of such law, as amended by chapter five fundred twenty-five of the laws of nineteen hundred fifty-three, is hereby amended to read as follows:

Subject to the general supervision and approval of the board of regents provision of the plan or general revision thereof proposed by the state university trustees as approved by the regents pursuant to section two hundred thirty-seven of this chapter, the state university trustees shall be responsible for:

6. The opening paragraph of subdivision two of section three hundred fifty-five of such law, as amended by chapter five hundred twenty-five of the laws of nineteen hundred fifty-three, is hereby amended to read as follows:

The state university trustees are further authorized and empowered, subject to the general supervision and approval of the board of regents provisions of the plan or general revision thereof proposed by the state university trustees as approved by the regents pursuant to section two hundred thirty-seven of this chapter:

7. Section sixty-two hundred two of such law, as last amended by a chapter of the laws of nineteen hundred sixty-one, entitled "An act to amend the education law, in relation to the number of regents college scholarships and scholarships for education in engineering and science, to establish the New York state scholar incentive program, to remove existing restrictions on the authority of the state university trustees, the contract colleges and the board of higher education in the city of New York to establish tuition policy and to repeal subdivision eight of section six hundred twelve-a thereof and making an appropriation therefor," is hereby amended to read as follows:

6202. Powers and duties

1. Such board of higher education shall be a separate and distinct body corporate, shall have the duties and powers of trustees of colleges as set forth in this chapter, unless otherwise specifically provided in this article, and the institutions and educational units which such board shall conduct shall be part of the common school system and shall have the powers and privileges of colleges and shall be subject to the visitation of the regents of the university. The control of the educational work of such institutions shall rest solely in the board of higher education. . . .

THE HARLEM RIOTS - 1964

From July 18 to July 22, 1964, a series of shootings, fires, street fights, and looting broke out in New York's predominantly black Harlem. Rioting has been no stranger to New York City, but the one in the long, hot summer of 1964 was one of the city's worst. The following selection describes the first day of the riot.

(Source: New York Times, July 19, 1964.)

Thousands of rioting Negroes raced through the center of Harlem last night and early today, shouting at policemen and white people, pulling fire alarms, breaking windows and looting stores.

At least 30 persons were arrested.

There was no estimate on the number injured. Scores of persons with bloodied heads were seen throughout the eight-block area between Eighth and Lenox Avenues and 123rd and 127th Streets, where most of the rioting occurred.

The riot grew out of a demonstration in front of the West 123rd Street police station protesting the slaying of a Negro youth by a white police lieutenant last Thursday.

The demonstration followed a rally at 125th Street and Seventh Avenue, where speakers decried the shooting of the boy, 15-year old James Powell, by Lieut. Thomas Gilligan in Yorkville.

Block Sealed Off

When the police sealed off the block in front of the station house, between Seventh and Eighth Avenues, the shouting, keyed-up crowd spread out in angry groups in the surrounding neighborhood.

Shots fired into the air by policemen to disperse the milling crowds echoed through streets littered with overturned garbage cans and broken glass.

More than 500 policemen, including all members of the tactical patrol force on dlty in Manhattan and Brooklyn, were called out to control the mobs. However, the crowds continued to grow as rumors of the rioting spread through the community.

Fire Equipment Used

Fire apparatus was brought in at 1 A.M. in an effort to block off streets in the riot area.

The Transit Authority sent extra policemen to stand guard at most of the Harlem subway stations. It also diverted buses from their regular routes.

By 3 A.M., five and a half hours after the riot started, the situation was not under control.

Police roamed the streets with revolvers drawn.

On Lenox Avenue, between 125th and 126th Streets, police fired at people who were throwing bottles and bricks down at them from roofs.

Some people milling at the corner of 125th Street and Lenox Avenue ran as the policemen fired. Others stood their ground, laughing and applauding.

Attempts to disperse the crowds by appealing to them through loud speakers failed.

"Why don't you go home," pleaded a policeman through a bull-horn on one block.

"We are home--this is our home," answered a person from a crowd.

Random eruptions of the disorders prevented the police from getting the situation under control. When the demonstration centered on the station house, they were able to control it.

Patrol cars with sirens screaming raced along the streets responding to "10-13's," the code call for assistance.

The Fire Department reported numerous false alarms. There were eight between 11 o'clock and midnight.

Cars Beaten On

Traffic was diverted because youths were stopping traffic to beat on cars and harangue drivers particularly if they were white. Windows were broken in at least one auto.

The crowds grew as one person told another of the earlier demonstration in front of the police station and of the alleged brutality employed by the police to break up the crowd there.

One rumor was that the police had seized a young man at random and beat him.

The young man was seized after a policeman, Michael Doris, was hit in the head with a bottle while trying to push back a crowd in front of the police station.

The young man shouted that "I didn't do it--you've got the wrong man" as the police pulled him into the station house.

"They're beating him--they're beating," the crowd shouted. As the crowd was dispersed the story spread.

Theater Crowd Told

A large group leaving the Apollo Theater on 125th Street heard it. So did persons leaving the IND subway station at Eighth Avenue and 125th Street.

At 1 A.M. the police were forced to bar all pedestrian traffic from 125th Street between Fifth and Eighth Avenues.

The windows in at least three stores on 125th Street were broken, and goods from window displays were stolen or thrown on the sidewalk. The police reported four persons had been arrested for burglary.

Some policemen patrolled the streets in civilian clothes with badges hanging from their pockets and with revolvers drawn.

Fires Set in Baskets

People from the area ran up and down the streets from group to group. Refuse baskets were set afire and molotov cocktail bombs, bottles filled with gasoline, were thrown into the streets.

More than 20 patrol cars had to come to the assistance of policemen at the corner of 125th Street and Lenox Avenue who were guarding two smashed shop windows when a group of Negroes began to threaten them.

The reinforcements dispersed the crowd by firing shots into the air. The crowd retreated, shouting taunts over their shoulders.

However, when the reinforcements left to assist other policemen, the crowd re-formed and threated the guards again. This maneuver was typical of the many roving gangs in the area.

Windshields of at least two police cars were smashed by hurled objects. Policemen of foot moved gingerly along the streets to avoid objects thrown from roofs.

Crowds even yelled "Killers, killers" at policemen who went to the aid of a young Negro girl who apparently was struck by a hit and run driver on 125th Street.

A march to the police station had been stirred by several speakers at the rally, held at Seventh Avenue and 125th Street by three chapters of the Congress of Racial Equality.

After persons representing CORE had spoden, the speakers platform, a kitchen chair, was turned over to speakers representing various other groups, including the United African Movement and the Harlem Progressive Labor Movement.

One of the last speakers, the Rev. Nelson C. Dukes of the Fountain Spring Baptist Church, 158 West 126th Street, called for the march on the station house to demand the arrest of Lieutenant Gilligan on a murder charge.

After the rally broke up at 8:45 P.M., Mr. Dukes led the crowd down Seventh Avenue to the station house. There it attempted to push its way in through the front door, but was blocked by five policement who locked their arms.

Then, with the help of reinforcements, the police pushed the crowd across the street. By this time, 9:30 o'clock, the block had filled with spectators.

As the police tried to contain the crowd, bottles and the covers of refuse cans rained down from roofs.

Patrolman Michael Doris, who was struck by a bottle, was taken to Sydenham Hospital. His condition was later reported as satisfactory.

A second patrolman, Frank Estrazza of the 34th precinct in the Bronx, was struck on the leg by a molotov cocktail on 125th Street near Seventh Avenue. He was treated at Knickerbocker Hospital and released.

A bus with patrolmen of the tactical force arrived to assist the police of the 28th Precinct to clear the block. There were several scuffles, with both policemen and demonstrators falling to the ground.

Those arrested were charged with disorderly conduct and resisting arrest after they sat down in the middle of the street and refused to move.

By 10 o'clock, the street had been cleared and barricades set up at the avenues. Policemen in riot helmets roamed the roofs and stood shoulder to shoulder at the barricades.

"Killer cops must go," shouted the crowd. "Police brutality must go. Murphy (Police Commissioner Michael J. Murphy) must go."

It was after the police had cleared 123rd Street and had pushed the mob into the avenues that the rioting began.

Assistant Chief Inspector Harry Taylor of the Manhattan North Borough Command headed police operations at the scene.

Many policemen due for dismissal on completion of their tours at midnight in Harlem precincts were ordered to remain on duty until otherwise instructed.

Besides the tactical patrol force, a motorcycle detail was sent into the area.

Throughout the evening routine calls for aid in upper Manhattan were going unheeded as the police concentrated their strength in the trouble spot.

Shortly after 1 A.M., the police announced that all persons arrested were to be taken to stations other than the one at West 123rd Street to reduce the possibility of the formation of new crowds there.

The men from the tactical patrol force sent to the scene are members of a group of about 200 handpicked men, all over six feet tall, all trained in judo and all under 30 years of age. The force was organized in 1958 as a roving unit that could be dispatched to danger areas.

Meanwhile, a group of Harlem leaders met at the 123rd Street station house with Deputy Police Commissioner Philip Walsh. Attending the meeting were Madison Jones, executive director of the City Commission on Human Rights, Criminal Court Judge Kenneth M. Phipps and James Lawson of the United African Nationalist Movement.

The group decided to ask Police Commissioner Michael J. Murphy to write a letter asking for law and order. The letter is to be read at all church services in Harlem this morning.

Fifteen of those arrested were taken to Manhattan Night Court early today, charged with disorderly conduct and resisting arrest. Nine of the demonstrators were paroled by Judge J. Howard Rossback. The six others were held in $500 bail, pending trial on Friday in Criminal Court.

Mr. Dukes was shaken by the developments. Speaking to a police officer, he said:

"If I knew this was going to happen, I would not have said anything."

There had been no incidents at the rally, which was attended by 250 persons. It was sponsored by the East River, Downtown and South Jamaica chapters of CORE.

"I belong to a nonviolent organization," Chris Sprownal, chairman of Downtown CORE told the crowd,"but I'm not nonviolent. When a cop shoots me, I will shoot him back."

The crowd responded with shouts such as "That's right, brother," and "Blood for blood."

BIBLIOGRAPHY

The following selected bibliography by no means exhausts the vast amount of written materials concerned with the history of New York City. However, the titles listed on the next few pages will be useful in enlarging the picture of New York City that has been presented in the foregoing pages.

At the time of this printing, no definitive history of New York City has been written. However, the many monographs already published provide the student interested in the subject with ample materials for his research. There is still a great deal to be done on the topic, and it is hoped that the future years will bring forth a host of materials on aspects of New York City's growth and development that have heretofore been neglected.

While this bibliography deals primarily with secondary sources, it should be understood that there are, readily available, literally mountains of primary papers and documents. Such collections as the Minutes of the Common Council, the Minutes of the Board of Aldermen, the Proclamations of the Mayor, Laws and Statutes of New York, Mayoralty Papers, Mayor's Annual Messages, Proceedings of the Council of the City of New York, Annual Reports of the Police Commissioner, Annual Reports of the Board of Education, and Annual Reports of the Board of Health are not only important, but also essential in doing research connected with New York City's history. Most of the large libraries in the city contain these materials: the New York Public Library, the New-York Historical Society Library, the Municipal Library, to name but a few. The author has deliberately omitted citations of this type, because of their numbers, and the lack of space in this volume.

To help the interested student, however, the last section of this bibliography lists a variety of bibliographies on New York City. It is the purpose of this book's bibliography section, like the chronology and documents sections, to act as a good starting point for pursuing the subject in greater depth and detail. The author has annotated some of the more important titles, so as to be of even greater aid to the researcher using this volume.

Abbott, Wilbur C. New York in the American Revolution, New York, 1912.

Albion, Robert G. The Rise of the New York Port (1815-1860). New York, 1939. One of the best books on the subject. Well written and documented.

Alexander, DeAlva Stanwood. Four Famous New Yorkers. Vol. 4 of a Political History of New York State, 1882-1905. New York, 1923. A detailed political history of New York City at the turn of the century.

Alexander, Edward. A Revolutionary Conservative: James Duane of New York. New York, 1947.

Allen, Robert S., ed. Our Fair City. New York, 1947.

Allen William H. Why Tammanies Revive: LaGuardia's Mis-Guard. New York, 1937. A slashing attack on the first LaGuardia administration.

Arm, Walter. Pay Off! The Inside Story of Big City Corruption. New York, 1951.

Asbury, Herbert. The Gangs of New York: An Informal History of the Underworld. New York, 1939. Politics and law enforcement emerge as interests of the New York City underworld in this study of criminal gangs.

Barck, Oscar T., Jr. New York City during the War for Independence. New York, 1931.

Beggs, Donald, ed. New York; The City That Belongs to the World. New York, 1956.

Bercovici, Konrad. Around the World in New York. New York, 1924.

Berger, Meyer. The Eight Million. New York, 1942.

--------------.The Story of the New York Times, New York, 1951. A reporter's history of a newspaper whose editorials and news columns have repeatedly affected the politics and policies of the city.

Berger, Meyer, and Busse, Fritz. New York: City on Many Waters. New York, 1955.

Blake, Nelson M. Water for the Cities. Syracuse, New York, 1956. Excellent, detailed study of an important aspect of urban growth.

Blanshard, Paul. "LaGuardia vs. McKee." The Nation. vol. 137. October, 1933.

Bleven, Bruce. Battle for Manhattan. New York, 1964. Interesting little book on New York during the Revolutionary War.

BIBLIOGRAPHY

Bogard, Milo T., ed. The Redemption of New York. New York, 1902. A review of the election of 1901 by New Yorkers who contributed to the victory of Seth Low.

Breen, William H. Thirty Years of New York Politics up to Date. New York, 1899. New York politics prior to and at the time of the city's consolidation.

Brown, Henry C. From Alley Pond to Rockefeller Center. New York, 1936.

──────────. The Story of Old New York. New York, 1940.

Bullock, William. "Hylan." American Mercury. vol. 1. April 1924. Tells about Hylan's rise over brains and personality.

Callow, Alexander. The Tweed Ring. New York, 1966.

Carlson, Oliver, and Bates, Ernest S. Hearst: Lord of San Simeon. New York, 1936. Biography of the famous publisher who was prominent in New York City politics for many years.

Chamberlain, John. "Mayor LaGuardia." Yale Review. vol. 29. September, 1939. The political personality of the mayor.

Child, Lydia. Letters From New York. New York, 1845.

Citizens Union. "An Appraisal of the Impellitteri Record." The Searchlight. vol. 42. May, 1952. Emphasizes the shortcoming of Impellitteri's administration.

──────────. Scrapbooks. 206 vols. Vols. 47-55. Covers the mayors of the City, 1922-1935. New York, 1936.

Conkling, Alfred R. City Government in the United States. New York, 1899. A former member of the Board of Aldermen touches on some aspects of city government in New York.

Cuneo, Ernest. Life with Fiorello. New York, 1955. An intimate portrait by a man who was closely associated with the mayor.

Davis, Elmer. History of the New York Times. New York, 1921. Contains many examples of how a newspaper can influence municipal government.

Durand, Edward D. The Finances of New York City. New York, 1898. Discusses the fiscal story of New York City from 1830 to 1897.

Dworkis, Martin B. The Impact of Puerto Rican Migration on Government Services in New York City. New York, 1957.

Earle, Alice. Colonial Days in Old New York. New York, 1937.

Edwards, George W. New York as an Eighteenth Century Municipality, 1731-1776. New York, 1917.

Ernst, Robert. Immigrant Life in New York City, 1825-1863. New York, 1949. One of the best books written on the subject. Brilliantly documented.

"Federal Writers' Project of the Works Progress Administration in New York City." New York City Guide. New York, 1939.

Fitch, Charles E., ed. Official New York from Cleveland to Hughes. 4 vols. New York, 1911.

Flick, Alexander C. History of the State of New York. 10 vols. New York, 1933-37.

——————————. Samuel J. Tilden. New York, 1939. Probably the best biography written about this famous New Yorker.

Flynn, Edward J. You're The Boss. New York, 1947.

Foner, Philip S. Business and Slavery: The New York Merchants and the Irrepressible Conflict. Chapel Hill, 1941. One of the most important and interesting books on this subject.

Foord, John. The Life and Public Services of Andrew Haswell Green. New York, 1913. A biography of the foremost champion of consolidation.

Fowler, Gene. Beau James: The Life and Times of Jimmy Walker. New York, 1949. A biography notable for its wealth of anecdotes.

Francis, John W. Old New York, or Reminiscences of the Past Sixty Years. New York, 1858.

Franklin, Jay. LaGuardia: A Biography. New York, 1937. Information about politics during LaGuardia's first administration.

Fuller, Hector. Abroad With Mayor Walker. New York, 1958. A eulogistic account of one phase of Mayor Walker's career.

Furer, Howard B. William Frederick Havemeyer: A Political Biography. New York, 1964.

Gavit, John P. "LaGuardia--Portrait of a Mayor." Survey Graphic. vol. 25. January, 1936.

Gibson, Florence E. The Attitudes of the New York Irish, Toward State and National Affairs, 1838-1892. New York, 1951.

Gittel, Marilyn, and Berube, Maurice R. Confrontation at Ocean Hill-Brownsville. New York, 1969. Excellent study of the New York school strikes of 1968.

Glazer, Nathan. "New York's Puerto Ricans." Commentary. Vol. 26. December, 1958.

Glazer, Nathan, and Moynihan, Daniel. Beyond the Melting Pot. Cambridge, 1963. Revisionist interpretation of the role New York City has played in assimilating immigrant groups.

Godkin, Edwin L. "Problems of Government." Annals of the American Academy of Political and Social Science. New York, 1894.

Gosnell, Harold F. Boss Platt and His New York Machine. Chicago, 1924. A turn of the century Republican state leader who exerted great influence on the city's Republican party.

Gover, William C. Tammany Hall Democracy of the City of New York. New York, 1875.

Graham, Frank. Al Smith, American. New York, 1945.

Greeley, Horace. Recollections of a Busy Life. New York, 1868.

Gribetz, Louis J., and Kaye, Joseph. Jimmie Walker: Story of a Personality. New York, 1932. A favorable view of the mayor.

Griscom, John H. Sanitary Condition of the Laboring Population of New York. New York, 1845. One of the first books of its kind, and a classic in its field.

Guernsey, R.S. New York City and Vicinity during the War of 1812-1815. 2 vols. New York, 1895.

Hall, Edward H. A Short Biography of Andrew Haswell Green. New York, 1904. This biography of the Father of Greater New York, traces the steps in the consolidation of the city.

Hamburger, Philip. Mayor Watching and Other Pleasures. New York, 1958. Personal observations of Mayors LaGuardia, O'Dwyer, Impellitteri, and Wagner.

----------------. "The Mayor: Profile of Robert F. Wagner." The New Yorker. vol. 32. January, February, 1957. Wagner's life and political career.

Handlin, Oscar. Al Smith and His America. Boston, 1958. Excellent biography of the colorful boy from the sidewalks of New York who rose to become governor.

Hapgood, Hutchins. The Spirit of the Ghetto. New York, 1902. Colorful, humorous account of the Jewish quarter in New York City at the turn of the century.

Hapgood, Norman, and Moscowitz, Henry. Up From the City Street: A Life of Alfred E. Smith. New York, 1928. Some phases of Mayor Hylan's career and personality are covered.

Harrington, Virginia. The New York Merchant on the Eve of the Revolution. New York, 1950.

Haswell, Charles H. Reminiscences of an Octogenarian of the City of New York, 1816-1860. New York, 1862.

Hawkins, Stuart. New York, New York. New York, 1957.

Headley, Joel T. The Great Riots of New York, 1712-1873. New York, 1873. Old, but valuable account.

Hirsch, Mark D. William C. Whitney: Modern Warwick. New York, 1948. The biography of a New Yorker prominent in municipal affairs in the nineteenth century.

Hockman, William R. William J. Gaynor: The Years of Fruition. Michigan, 1955. A detailed biography of a mayor based on a careful study of original sources.

Howe, Wirt. New York at the Turn of the Century: 1899-1916. Toronto, 1916. Republican politics in the newly consolidated city.

Hylan, John F. Autobiography. New York, 1922.

Impellitteri, Vincent R. Scrapbooks. 2 vols. 1950. Newspaper clippings relating chiefly to the period when Impellitteri was acting mayor.

Ingersoll, Raymond V. "An Estimate of Mayor Gaynor." National Municipal Review. vol. 3. January, 1914.

Innes, John H. New Amsterdam and its People. New York, 1937.

Isaacs, Julius. Oath of Devotion. New York, 1949. A public official relates his story.

Ivins, William M. Machine Politics and Money in Elections in New York City. New York, 1887. An authoritative and incisive volume which reveals much about politics in the city.

Jameson, J. Franklin, ed. Narrative of New Netherlands, 1609-1664. New York, 1909.

Janvier, Thomas A. In Old New York. New York, 1894.

Johnson, James Weldon. Black Manhattan. New York, 1930.

Johnston, Alva. "The Scholar in Politics: Profile of Mayor John P. O'Brien." The New Yorker. vol. 9. July, 1933. Portrait of O'Brien as one of the choicest flowers of Tammany Hall.

July, Robert. Essential New Yorker: Gulian C. Verplanck. North Carolina, 1951.

Kapp, Friedrich. Immigration and the Commissioners of Emigration of the State of New York. New York, 1870.

Kefauver, Estes. Crime in America. New York. 1951.

Kennedy, Albert G. Social Settlements in New York City, their Activities, Policies and Administration. New York. 1925.

Kenworthy, E.W. "The Emergence of Mayor Wagner." The New York Times Magazine. August 14, 1955.

King, Moses, ed., King's Handbook of New York City. Buffalo, 1893.

Klein, Alexander, ed., The Empire City. New York, 1955.

Kneeland, George J. Commercialized Prostitution in New York City. New York, 1917.

Kong, Chew-Kawn. The Role of the City Administrator in New York City. New York, 1958. A study of the evolution and functioning of the city administrator's office in New York.

Kouwenhoven, John. Columbia Portrait of New York City. New York, 1951. Excellent pictorial history of New York.

LaGuardia, Fiorello H. The Making of an Insurgent. Philadelphia, 1948. The mayor's autobiography to the year 1919.

Lamb, Martha. History of New York City. 2 vols. New York, 1880. Old, but still valuable account of the history of the city.

Lanier, Henry W. A Century of Banking in New York. New York, 1923.

Lavine, Emmanuel H. Secrets of the Metropolitan Police. New York, 1937. Describes links between criminals and the police.

Leonard, John W. The History of New York City. New York, 1910.

Lewis, Alfred H. Richard Croker. New York, 1930. Good biography of a Tammany Hall leader.

Leyson, Burr W. Fighting Crime: the New York Police Department in Action. New York, 1935.

Limpus, Lowell M. History of the New York Fire Department. New York 1936.

Limpus, Lowell M., and Leyson, Burr W. This Man LaGuardia. New York, 1938. A full scale biography of the mayor.

Lindsay, John V. The City. New York, 1970. An attempt by the mayor to explain his administrations.

Lossing, Benson J. History of New York City. New York, 1884.

Low, Benjamin R.C. Seth Low. New York, 1955. The career of Greater New York's second mayor by a relative.

Low, Seth. Papers. Seth Low Collection. Low Library, Columbia University. Letters and manuscript material.

Lowi, Theodore J. At The Pleasure of the Mayor. New York, 1962. An excellent study of mayors' cabinets in New York from Van Wyck to Wagner.

Lundberg, Ferdinand. Imperial Hearst: A Social Biography. New York, 1936.

Luthin, Richard H. American Demagogues: Twentieth Century. Boston, 1954. A detailed portrait of Vito Marcantonio.

Lydenberg, Harry M. History of the New York Public Library. New York, 1923.

Lynch, Dennis T. Boss Tweed. New York, 1927. Classic study of Tweed, but out of date.

------------. Criminals and Politicians. New York, 1932. How criminals have attempted to influence office holders in New York City.

Mack, Edward C. Peter Cooper, Citizen of New York. New York, 1949.

MacKaye, Milton A. The Tin Box Parade: A Handbook for Larceny. New York, 1934. Journalistic sketches of public figures and political personalities.

MacLeod, Donald. Biography of Honorable Fernando Wood. New York, 1856. Old, but still valuable work on a scoundrel.

Mandelbaum, Seymour. Boss Tweed's New York. New York, 1965.

Mann, Arthur. LaGuardia: A Fighter Against His Times, 1882-1933. Philadelphia, 1959. First volume of the definitive biography of LaGuardia.

Markey, Morris. Manhattan Reporter. New York, 1935.

Matthews, James M. Recollections of Persons and Events Chiefly in the City of New York. New York, 1865.

McAdoo, William. Guarding a Great City. New York, 1906. The recollections of a police commissioner.

McClellan, George B. Jr. Papers. Library of Congress, Washington, D.C. The collected papers of the mayor, 1904-1909.

McGoldrick, Joseph D. "Our American Mayors: Jimmy Walker." National Municipal Review. vol. 17. October 1928. An appraisal of Mayor Walker during his first administration.

McGurrin, James. Burke Cochran: A Freelance in American Politics. New York, 1948. A biography of a Tammany leader.

Mitgang, Herbert. The Man Who Rode The Tiger. New York, 1970. Excellent work concerned with the Seabury investigation of Mayor Walker's administrations.

Mockridge, Norton, and Prall, Robert H. The Big Fix. New York, 1954. The story of District Attorney Miles McDonald and Mayor O'Dwyer.

Monaghan, Frank, and Lowenthal, Marvin. This was New York; The Nation's Capital in 1789. New York, 1952.

Morris, Charles. Men of Affairs in New York: An Historical Work. New York, 1906.

Morris, Lloyd. Incredible New York. New York, 1951.

Morris, Newbold, and Thomas Dana L. Let the Chips Fall. New York, 1955. Recollections of a former alderman and president of the City Council.

Moscow, Warren. Politics in the Empire State. New York, 1948. A pungent account of LaGuardia's administrations as mayor.

Moses, Robert. A Salute and a Memoir. New York, 1957. A member of

LaGuardia's official family writes about the mayor.

Myers, Gustavus. The History of Tammany Hall. New York, 1917. Old, but still contains valuable information, although laudatory.

Neufeld, Ernst, ed. The Renascence of City Hall. New York, 1956.

Nevins, Allan, ed. The Diary of Philip Hone. 2 vols. New York, 1936. Contains much important information and commentary.

------------. The Evening Post: A Century of Journalism. New York, 1922. An excellent history of the famous New York Newspaper.

Nevins, Allan, and Krout, John A., eds. The Greater City: New York, 1898-1948. New York, 1948. The story of the city's consolidation, its early years, and its development.

Nevins, Allan, and Thomas, Milton H., eds. The Diary of George Templeton Strong. 4 vols. New York, 1952.

Northrop, W.B., ed. Some of Mayor Gaynor's Letters and Speeches. New York, 1913. Mayor Gaynor's views on a variety of things.

O'Brien, Frank M. The Story of the Sun: 1833-1928. New York, 1928. A history of an influential city newspaper.

O'Callaghen, E.B. ed. The Documentary History of the State of New York. 4 vols. Albany, 1950-51.

O'Connor, Richard. Hell's Kitchen. Philadelphia, 1958.

Odell, George C.D. Annals of the New York Stage. 14 vols. New York, 1927-1945.

O'Dwyer, William. Papers. Municipal Archives, New York City, 1932-1957.

Osgood, Samuel. New York in the Nineteenth Century. New York, 1910.

Osofsky, Gilbert. Harlem: The Making of a Ghetto. New York, 1966. One of the best books on the subject.

Paltsits, Victor H. "The Founding of New Amsterdam in 1626." Proceedings of the American Antiquarian Society. XXXIV. April, 1924.

Parkhurst, C.H. My Forty Years in New York. New York, 1923. The life story of one reformer who fought Tammany Hall.

Peterson, Arthur E. New York as an eighteenth Century Muncipality prior to 1731. New York, 1898.

Pink, Louis H. Gaynor: The Man Who Swallowed the Tiger. New York, 1931. A very sympathetic biography of the mayor.

Pintard, John. Letters From John Pintard to His Daughter, 1816-1833. New York, 1932.

Pleasants, Samuel A. Fernando Wood of New York. New York, 1948. Excellent, scholarly biography of Mayor Wood.

Pomerantz, Sidney I. New York an American City, 1783-1803. New York, 1938.

Raesly, Ellis L. Portrait of New Netherland. New York, 1945.

Rand, Christopher. The Puerto Ricans. New York, 1958.

Rankin, Rebecca B., ed. New York Advancing: Seven More Years of Progressive Administration in the City of New York, 1939-1945. New York, 1945.

──────────────. New York Advancing: A Scientific Approach to Municipal Government. New York, 1936.

Reid, Edward. The Shame of New York. New York, 1953. Exposes Connections between crime and politics in New York City.

Richardson, James. History of the New York Police Department. New York, 1971. Modern, scholarly study.

Richmond, J.E. New York and Its Institutions. New York, 1873.

Riesenberg, Felix. Portrait of New York. New York, 1939.

Rodgers, Cleveland. Robert Moses: Builder for Democracy. New York, 1952. Solid biography of a dynamic city administrator. Contains aspects of various city administrations.

Rodgers, Cleveland, and Rankin, Rebecca B. New York: The World's Capital City. New York, 1948.

Rosario-Nieves, Luis. Puerto Ricans in New York City from 1910-1950. New York, 1952.

Rosenberg, Charles. The Cholera Years. Chicago, 1962. Very well done study of the epidemics of 1832, 1849 and 1866 in New York City.

Rothery, Agnes E. New York Today. New York, 1951.

Sayre, Wallace S., and Kaufman, Herbert. Governing New York City: Politics in the Metropolis. New York, 1956. Excellent study of the governmental process in New York from consolidation through the Wagner administrations.

Scheiner, Seth. Negro Mecca. New York, 1965.

Schneider, David M. History of Public Welfare in New York State, 1609-1866. Chicago, 1938.

Scisco, Louis D. Political Nativism in New York State. New York, 1901. Old, but very useful as far as it goes.

Sexton, Patricia Cayo. Spanish Harlem. New York, 1965. Fascinating book on a new culture within the city.

Shaw, Frederick. History of the New York City Legislature. New York, 1954. Includes discussion of the Old Board of Aldermen before consolidation.

Shepherd, William R. The Story of New Amsterdam. New York, 1926. Informative, interesting work of the Dutch period.

Sherman, Phileman T. Inside the Machine: Two Years in the Board of Aldermen, 1898-1899. New York, 1901.

Simon, Kate. New York Places and Pleasures. New York, 1959.

Singleton, Esther. "History of the Opera in New York from 1750 to 1898." Musical Courier. December, 1898.

Smith, Mortimer. William Jay Gaynor: Mayor of New York. Chicago, 1951. Excellent biography, although too complimentary at times.

Spaulding, E. Wilder. New York in the Critical Period, 1783-1789. New York, 1963.

Steffens, Lincoln. Autobiography. New York, 1931. A great reporter views the administration of Mayor Seth Low.

———————. The Shame of the Cities. New York, 1957. Excellent view of New York City particularly political corruption.

Stevens, John A. The Union Defense Committee of the City of New York. New York, 1862.

Stiles, Henry M., ed. The History of the County of Kings and the City of Brooklyn, New York from 1683-1884. 2 vols. New York, 1884.

Still, Bayrd. Mirror for Gotham: New York as seen by Contemporaries, Dutch Days to the Present. New York, 1956. Very interesting work, with contemporary writings blended into the narrative.

Stokes, I.N. Phelps. New York Past and Present. New York, 1939.

----------------------, ed. The Iconography of Manhattan Island, 1498-1909. 6 vols. New York, 1915-1926. A day to day description of all the important events in the history of the city. Excellent maps, plates, and reproductions.

Street, Julian. "New York's Fighting Mayor." Collier's Weekly. vol. 59. August, 1917. A favorable view of Mayor Mitchell's administration.

Syrett, Harold. The City of Brooklyn, 1865-1898. New York, 1944. Solid history of Brooklyn as far as it goes.

------------, ed. The Gentleman and the Tiger: The Autobiography of George B. McClellan Jr. Philadelphia, 1956. The memoirs of the third mayor after consolidation.

Thompson, D.G. Brinton. Ruggles of New York, New York, 1946.

Tilden, Samuel J. The New York City Ring. New York, 1873.

Townshend, John D. New York in Bondage. New York, 1901. An unfriendly view of Tammany and its operations.

Trachtenberg, Alan. Brooklyn Bridge. New York, 1965. The best work on the subject. Scholarly written.

Tunnard, Christopher, and Reed, Henry H. American Skyline. New York, 1953.

Valentine, Lewis Jr. Police Night Stick. New York, 1947. Interesting autobiography of a Police Commissioner.

Van Pelt, Daniel. Leslie's History of Greater New York. 2 vols. New York, 1899.

Van Wyck, Frederick. Recollections of an Old New Yorker. New York, 1932. Recollections of a cousin of the first mayor of the Greater City.

Ware, Caroline F. Greenwich Village, 1920-1930. New York, 1935.

Werner, Morris R. It Happened in New York. New York, 1957.

----------------. Tammany Hall. New York, 1928. Good study of the growth and development of Tammany, although not particularly scholarly.

Wertenbaker, Thomas J. Father Knickerbocker Rebels. New York, 1948.

Whalen, Grover. Mr. New York: The Autobiography of Grover Whalen. New York, 1955.

White, E.B. Here is New York. New York, 1949.

Wilson, James G., ed. Memorial History of the City of New York. 4 vols. New York, 1892-1893. A very good study as far as it goes.

Winkler, John K. William Randolph Hearst. New York, 1955. Most up to date biography of the influential publisher.

Zeller, Belle. Pressure Politics in New York. New York, 1937. A study of group representation before the State Legislature.

Zinn, Howard. Fiorello LaGuardia in Congress. Michigan, 1958.

BIBLIOGRAPHIES ON NEW YORK CITY

Brooklyn Public Library List of Books on Greater New York in the Brooklyn Public Library. 3rd ed. The Library, Brooklyn, 1909.

Dunn, James T., "Masters' Thesis and Doctoral Dissertations in New York History (1897-1951)," New York History. vol. 33, 1952.

Eiberson, Harold, and Ditzion, Sidney, "Sources for the Study of the New York Area: A Bibliographic Essay." The New York Area Research Council, City College, New York, 1957.

Government Affairs Foundation Metropolitan Communities: A Bibliography. Public Administration Service, Chicago, 1956.

Institute of Public Administration Selected Recent References on Materials Relating to the Operation of the Government of the City of New York. The Institute, New York, 1959.

Municipal Reference Library Notes, 1914 to Date (Indexed).

New-York Historical Society "Books about New York City, Primarily History, Published from 1898-1947." The Society, New York, 1948.

New York Public Library "Selected List of Works Relating to City Planning and Allied Subjects," New York Public Library Bulletin, vol. 17, 1913.

Port of New York Authority A Selected Bibliography of the Port of New York Authority, 1921 to 1956. The Authority, New York, 1957.

Reynolds, James B., ed. Civic Bibliography for Greater New York. Charities Publication Committee, New York, 1911.

Selected Bibliography on Revision of the New York City Charter. School of Public Affairs, Princeton, N. J., 1933.

Shaw, Thomas S. Index to Profile Sketches in the New Yorker Magazine. Boston, 1946.

Spielvogel, Samuel A Selected Bibliography on City and Regional Planning. Washington, 1951.

United States Works Progress Administration, Division of Professional and Service Projects Guide to Manuscript Depositories in New York City. Historical Records Survey, New York, 1941.

Vormalker, Rose L. Special Library Resources. Special Libraries Association, New York, 1941.

NAME INDEX

Allen, Stephen, 23
Amen, John Harlan, 45
Andros, Edmund, 9, 10, 11
Archer, John, 8
Astor, John Jacob, 29

Barnum, P.T., 29
Barsimson, Jacob, 5
Bartholdi, Frederic, 35
Beame, Abraham, 54
Bedloe, Isaac, 9
Bennett, James Gordon, 25
Bernhardt, Sarah, 35
Bingham, Jonathan B., 51
Bingham, R., 39
Block, Adriaen, 1
Bowne, Walter, 24
Bradford, William, 13
Brady, William V., 28
Brockholls, Anthony, 10
Bronck, James, 3
Buckley, Charles A., 51
Burnet, William, 12, 13
Burr, Aaron, 18

Carnegie, Andrew, 38
Christenberry, Robert K., 48
Clark, Aaron, 26
Clark, George, 13
Clemenceau, Georges, 41
Clinton, De Witt, 21, 22
Clinton, George, 14
Colden, Cadwallader, 15, 23
Colles, Christopher, 16
Colve, Anthony, 9
Coman, Thomas, 32
Cortelyou, Jacques, 6
Cosby, William, 13

de Forest, Hendrick, 6
de Koningh, Frederick, 6
DeLancey, James, 14, 15
Delanoy, Peter, 11
DeSapio, Carmine, 50, 51
de Sitte, Nicasius, 6
Dewey, Thomas E., 44, 45
Dickens, Charles, 27, 32

Dongan, Thomas, 10
Duane, James, 18, 19

Earl of Bellomont, 12
Earl of Dunmore, 16
Edison, Franklin, 35
Edison, Thomas, 35
Ellsler, Fanny, 27
Ely, Smith, 34
Embury, Philip, 15

Farley, Thomas M. 43
Farragut, David G., 35
Ferguson, John, 22, 23
Fisk, James, 32
Flagg, Ernest, 37
Fletcher, Benjamin, 11, 12
Foch, Ferdinand, 41
Forrest, Edwin, 29
Fulton, Robert, 21

Garibaldi, Guiseppi, 29
Garrison, William Lloyd, 25
Gaynor, William J., 39, 40
Geraedy, Philip, 3
Geritsen, Wolfert, 2
Gilbert, Cass, 40
Gilder, Richard W., 37
Gilroy, Thomas G., 36
Gould, Jay, 32
Grace, William R., 34
Graham, John, 10
Grant, Hugh J., 36
Greeley, Horace, 27
Griscom, John H., 27
Gross, Calvin, 51
Gunther, C. Godfrey, 31

Hale, Nathan, 17
Hall, A. Oakey, 33
Halley, Rudolph, 48
Hardy, Charles, 14
Harper, James, 28
Harriden, William F., 27
Hart, Eli, 26
Harvey, Charles, 32

Havemeyer, William F., 28, 33, 34
Hewitt, Abram S., 36
Hoffmann, John T., 32
Hone, Philip, 24
Hosack, David, 20, 21
Hudson, Henry, 1
Hughes, Charles Evans, 39
Hunter, Robert, 12
Hyde, Edwin, 12
Hylan, John F., 41

Impelliteri, Vincent R., 47
Ingoldsby, Richard ll, 12

Jack, Hulan, 49
Jackson, Andrew, 26
James, Duke of York, 7
Jans, Annetje, 2
Jans, Roeloff, 2
Jansen, Gerrit, 2
Johnson, Samuel, 14
Jones, George, 33

Kemble, Fanny, 25
Kieft, Wilhelm, 3, 4
King Charles II, 7
King George III, 16, 17
King James II, 11
King, Martin Luther, Jr., 53
King William IV, 17
Kingsland, Ambrose C., 29
Knapp, Whitman, 54
Kossuth, Louis, 29
Krol, Bastiaen Jansean, 2

• LaGuardia, Fiorello H., 43, 44, 45, 46, 47
Langtry, Lily, 35
Lawrence, Cornelius, 25
Lee, Charles, 17
Lee, Gideon, 25
Lee, Robert E., 31
Lefkowitz, Louis J., 50
Lehman, Herbert, 44, 45
Leisler, Jacob, 11

L'Enfant, Charles Pierre, 19
Levitt, Arthur, 50
Lincoln, Abraham, 30, 31
Lind, Jenny, 29
Lindburgh, Charles A., 42
Lindsay, John V., 52, 53, 54, 55
Livingston, Edward, 20, 21
Lovelace, Francis, 8, 9
Lovelace, John, 12
Low, Seth, 38

Macready, William, 29
Mangin, Joseph F., 21
Manning, Richard, 9
Marchi, John, 54
May, Cornelius Jacoben, 1
McClellan, George B., 31
McClellan, George B., Jr., 38, 39
McComb, John, Jr., 21
McKee, Joseph V., 43
McKinley, William, 37
Michelius, Jonas, 2
Mickle, Andrew H., 28
Milbourne, Jacob, 11
Minuit, Peter, 2
Mitchell, John Purroy, 39, 40
Mitchell, Samuel L., 21
Monckton, Robert, 15
Montgomerie, John, 13
Moore, Henry, 15
Morris, Robert H., 27
Morse, Samuel F.B., 26
Moses, Robert, 49
Murphy, Patrick V., 54

Nast, Thomas, 33
Nicolls, Matthias, 9, 10
Nicolls, Richard, 7, 8

O'Brien, John P., 43
O'Dwyer, William, 46, 47
Olmsted, Frederick L., 30
Opdyke, George, 31
Osborn, Danvers, 14

Paulding, William, 24
Pecora, Ferdinand, 47

NAME INDEX

Peeck, Jan, 6
Pintard, John, 21
Pitt, William, 16
Pluvier, Cornelius, 9
Polk, Frank L., 40
Powell, Adam Clayton, 52

Radcliffe, Jacob, 22, 23
Riegelmann, Harold, 48
Robertson, James, 17, 18
Rockefeller, Nelson, 49
Roelantsen, Adam, 2
Roosevelt, Franklin D., 43, 45
Ruggles, Samuel, 24

Samuels, Howard, 54
Scribner, Harvey, 54
Seabury, Samuel, 42-43
Slaughter, Henry, 11
Smith, William, 14
Stevens, John, 24
Strong, William L., 37
Stuyvesant, Peter, 4, 5, 6, 7, 9

Thacher, Thomas D., 44
Tiemann, Daniel F., 30
Truman, Harry S, 47
Tryon, William, 16, 17
Tweed, William Marcy, 33

Usselinx, William, 1

Valentine, David T., 27

Vance, Samuel B., 34
Van Curler, Jacobus, 2
Van Dam, Rip, 13
vander Donck, Adriaen, 5
Varian, Isaac L., 27
Varick, Richard, 19, 20
Van Twiller, Wouter, 2
Van Wyck, Robert A., 37
Vaux, Calvert, 30
Verhulst, William, 1
Verrazano, Giovanni de, 1
Vries, David Pietersz de, 3

Wagner, Robert F., 48, 49, 50, 51
Walker, James J., 41, 42, 43
Warburg, Felix, 47
Ware, James E., 34
Washington, George, 17, 18, 19
Westervelt, Jacob A., 29
White, Stanford, 37
Wickham, William H., 34
Willet, Thomas, 8
Willett, Marius, 21
William and Mary, 11
Wolfe, James, 15
Wood, Fernando, 29, 30
Woodhull, Caleb S., 29
Wright, Wilbur, 39

Zenger, John Peter, 13